You may contact Dr. Mike to discuss *Fix Your Family*, to seek some good advice, or to invite him to conduct a presentation at your location at

goodadvicedoctormike@gmail.com

(336) 257-9276

Praise for *Fix Your Family*
Dr. Mike Simpson

I can imagine no better teacher and mentor on the path of systems theory than Mike Simpson. With his characteristic playfulness, he delivered big lessons in an enjoyable and understandable way. Mike thoroughly delighted systems theory and taught me to engage in the process of examining family systems with an attitude of discovery, and even, pleasure. He provided tools to equip me in my comprehension of present circumstances by exploring past triumphs and errors, and he did this without condemnation. As I emerged from his workshops with a framework of understanding, Mike helped me to embrace the possibility of a future determined by my own desires and directions. What a gift it has been to learn from Dr. Mike Simpson!
—Rev. April McClure Stewart, Christian Minister

About twenty years ago, Dr. Mike Simpson introduced me to the concepts of Family Systems Theory, and my life has never been the same. His enthusiasm for this way of seeing the world—and that's what Bowen Family Systems theory is, a way of seeing the world—was contagious, and his passionate teaching style extremely effective. This little book puts the ideas of Bowen theory into the hands of anyone who might be motivated to help families be healthier and relationships more authentic. He describes these principles and their implications in plain English in an accessible, even humorous, way, going beyond introduction and launching them in a daring new direction. If you want your life to stay just like it is, don't, under any circumstances, read this book.
—Rev. Dennis Lundblad
Christian Minister; Lecturer, UNC Asheville

I was first introduced to Family Systems in 2001 when I attended a weekend retreat led by Mike Simpson. That weekend transformed how I understand myself and my family. Since that time, through continued study and practice, I have improved all of my relationships—not only those in my family, but also professionally. As I continue to grow, I am less afraid of conflict, I understand it's true source, and am able to address it to the benefit of not only myself, but all involved. Thank you, Mike Simpson, for teaching this unteachable, stubborn, resistant soul! I will be forever grateful!

—Rev. Melissa Ebken
Pastor, Illiopolis and Niantic Christian Churches

That Mike would eventually turn his attention to helping others solve deep seated problems within their families should be no surprise. For decades, as a pastor, he has assisted individuals and families and draws on a wealth of experience. *Fix Your Family* shares with us all the secrets that he has practiced as a counselor, leader, husband, father and family member. It is a valuable resource to help our families become more of what we truly desire them to be. Family is our circle of most loved, valued relationships. We do not always give the most careful thought as we try to fix things that are broken in our families, but with *Fix Your Family* a way forward is provided. Mike Simpson is a man of great depth, compassion, insight, faith, and gifts. What he shares with us is well worth the journey and I could not be more pleased than to commend his work to you.

—Rev. Rex Horne
Christian Church in North Carolina Regional Minister, Ret.

"Bowen's Family Systems Theory" (BFST) is not about espousing techniques. It is about operating with intentionality at a more conscious level and offers a framework for seeking answers within oneself. Family systems training is helping others **to see themselves as the key** to what happens within an emotional system. This book helps a reader understand the dynamics of doing just that. Ten years of regularly watching Simpson teach BSFT participants in retreat settings qualifies me to say: Simpson is a master teacher of BFST!

—Gwen Simmons, Ed.D.
Dean of Students, UNC Pembroke, Ret.

Fix Your Family

And Claim All the Power, Peace and Happiness You Can Handle

By

Dr. Mike Simpson

Clear Light Books
Indigo Sea Press
Winston-Salem

Indigo Sea Press
302 Ricks Drive
Winston-Salem, NC 27103
This book is a work of non-fiction. The author is solely responsible for the content, ideas and various materials contained in the manuscript. All identities of living individuals have been changed for the protection of privacy.

Copyright 2025 by Dr. Mike Simpson
All rights reserved, including the right of reproduction in whole or part in any format.
First Indigo Sea Press edition published
January, 2017
Moon Sailor and all production design
are trademarks of Indigo Sea Press, used under license.

For information regarding bulk purchases of this book, digital purchase and special discounts, please contact the publisher at indigoseapress@gmail.com

Cover design by Pan Morelli
Manufactured in the United States of America
ISBN 978-1-63066-464-0

To Murray, Ed and Lynda
and my other great teachers.

Acknowledgements

As you read *Fix Your Family*, a few names will appear with regularity—especially Ed Friedman and Murray Bowen. Obviously, since I'm "third generation" Family Systems, I'm totally indebted to these particular men (I was going to say "giants," but they would never have stood for that).

In writing the text, I found myself remembering a great many other folks who made my original Bowen Theory work possible. Close at hand, I am especially thankful to the late Lynda Tamblyn, fellow displaced Okie, whose quiet wisdom guided so much of our early work. Also to the wonderful Laura Tebow, who not only made those first Lazarus Project retreats possible, but also edited and proofed the rough draft of this book. Thanks to First Christian Church of Greensboro and First Christian of Winston-Salem, who gave me time away from the pastorate to work with other congregations and their leaders. Certain denominational leaders were extremely helpful, in particular Rex Horne of North Carolina and Burley Herron of Illinois. Other organizations were also open to the possibilities of empowerment that Emotional Process held for them, especially the Delta Kappa Gamma society in North Carolina. The individual who took Family Systems to the next step, a former DKG President and lifetime educator is Dr. Gwen Simmons, the author of *See Jane Not Run*, a marvelous book extending these theories to the classroom.

I would like to express my appreciation to some delightful colleagues who came on board first as participants in Family Systems workshops and then became my teachers. Rev. April McClure Stewart, Rev. Melissa Meers Ebken, Rev. Marcy Reid-Smith, Rev. Torrey Osgood and Rev. Dennis Lundblad, who coined the term "river of emotion." I found it not at all unusual to be leading a seminar and have these characters take over and offer new insights that were brilliant. I am in their debt. And to the marvelous facilitators, seminar participants and the families I've worked with going back to 1991 who helped me understand and share the insights collected here, I am grateful beyond anything I can express in words.

—Mike Simpson

Contents

1	Do You Have to Be So Emotional?	1
2	Your Family: Booby Traps or Buried Treasure?	23
3	Who Are These Strange People (I've Known All My Life)?	45
4	The Person in the Mirror Is the One You're Looking For	73
5	Arming, Planting and Detonating the Love Bomb	112
6	A Brief, Personal History	143
	Addendum 1: Crisis	160
	Addendum 2: Preserving Yesterday for Tomorrow	163
	Index	167
	For Further Reading	169
	Endnotes	170

1
Do You Have to Be So Emotional?

[Lots of times people who are under stress or in crisis pick up a book with a promising title and hurriedly look through the pages, observe how detailed or complex it seems at first, then set it down in disappointment. To help you with deciding whether this book can be useful or not, I've made a list at the end of each chapter (pages 21, 44, 71, 111, 141) that simply spells out what we've covered in that chapter. It's no substitute for reading all the insights and examples, but it does summarize why this book can help you fix your family.]

Long decades ago, when I first became interested in investigating problems within families and the possibility they could be healed, I read about four people—mom and dad, son and daughter—who were referred to a counselor for family therapy. Within only a couple of minutes, the counselor discerned a repetitive pattern in the way they related to one another: the younger child, a girl who spoke with a profound lisp, would excitedly say something and her brother would immediately begin to mock her, imitating her lisp; the father would yell angrily at the boy, frequently slapping him on the head; and the mother would begin to cry.

See, you feel better about your family already, don't you?

Our families can be the source of great joy, inspiration, sustenance and good examples of mercy and strength. It is possible a family can be all that. It's equally, painfully true that families can be our greatest source of misery, stagnation, anger and resentment. If you are reading a book titled *Fix Your Family*, chances are you're mostly likely well-acquainted with the ways in which your family doesn't work, the ways in which they come up short of being a joyous source of empowerment for you.

I'm guessing you know pretty well that families can be inadequate, dysfunctional fountains of pain. For you perhaps the real question is: can families be fixed? Is it possible the same family that turns every birthday, every holiday, maybe every meal into a nightmare can be transformed into a group of compassionate, accepting, sincere, nurturing loved ones?

It can happen, yes. Whether or not it will happen depends on your willingness to understand why they act as they do, to engage them, to persist in being part of their lives and, above all, to let yourself be empowered by what you're about to learn as you move through this process in order to fix your family.

Also, briefly I want to address the possibility of **crisis**. It might be you are experiencing a crisis in your family life. Maybe that's why you picked up this book. In a moment of family crisis, the situation we are facing so completely dominates our lives we cannot focus successfully on anything else. Before our normal lives can be resumed, we must solve the crisis. When a spouse abruptly leaves or threatens to abandon you; when a child becomes suicidal or is found to be on drugs; when a huge dispute—maybe it got physical or there was the threat of violence—has torn apart the family, it is also disrupting the stability, purpose and security we all depend upon simply to live day-to-day.

If you are in a crisis right now, having lived through them myself and having worked with hundreds of individuals and families in crisis, my first and best advice is that you take care of yourself first: make sure of your own safety and nurture, and then the safety and well-being of the dependent people for whom you care. Second, you may find a bit of insight if you skip over to Addendum 1 of this book, which is devoted to addressing crisis situations. In going straight there, you are passing over a great deal of useful information that will serve you as you work to renew your family. It's difficult, however, to take in new ideas and to develop new ways of relating to people when you are in crisis. As the saying goes, "When you're up to your elbows in alligators, you forget that your priority was to drain the swamp."

After you have gotten to a place of relief, there is one other observation I would make. It may seem more annoying than helpful at this particular moment, but six days or six weeks down the road it may make more sense. *The issues that perpetuated the crisis were in the family before it erupted* and, *despite appearances to the contrary, they are still present in the family.*

This book is designed to help root out the seeds of future crises so you never have to endure them again.

The ideas, insights and methods described in this book are not about therapy or diagnosis. This book presents a totally new framework for understanding yourself and your family and for interacting with your loved ones in entirely different ways. You will ask: "Are these ideas—that will often sound completely counterintuitive—really true and correct?" The short answer is yes. I have found these after thirty-five years of practicing and honing them, to be right on target. If they don't work for you, I'd like to hear about it. Ed Friedman used to joking say, "These ideas are right 70% of the time." Frankly, no one can guarantee an outcome because families are made up of people who are subject to deciding for themselves how they will respond to you. The insights shared here, as you may find, are spot on. This book (unless you got an autographed first edition maybe) certainly cost you less than any counseling session, divorce attorney or drug regimen you'll ever endure; and it's a whole lot more fun. Let's face it, there's probably not much you can say or do that will make your family function *worse* than it already does. So let's give this a try.

A Brief Emotional Catastrophe

Tied 1-1 at the end of the ninety-minute regulation period and almost two-thirds of way through the extra time (overtime) period, the two exhausted and frustrated soccer teams could see they were facing a penalty shootout to determine the winner. Then it happened.

Two players—each of whom had scored his team's goal during the match—were jogging down the field side-by-side. One of the two, a defender, said something to his opponent, a striker. The striker suddenly turned toward the defender and head-butted him in the chest. The defender, of course, responded in the usual manner of most professional soccer players: he screamed as if in excruciating pain and collapsed, apparently mortally injured. Up trotted the referee, waving a red card. The head-butting striker was immediately ejected. The defender, of course, leaped to his feet miraculously and continue playing—even without emergency medical attention.

Dr. Mike Simpson

So what? A soccer player responded angrily to something an opponent said, foolishly butted him and got kicked out of the match. Was it really that big a deal?

It was a very big deal. This soccer (or as the majority of humanity calls it, "football") match was the FIFA World Cup Championship: Italy vs. France in Berlin, July 9, 2006. Soccer is the most passionately, universally loved sport in the world; and the ultimate championship in soccer is the quadrennial FIFA World Cup. This notorious head-butting incident is one of the most unforgettable, game-changing, stupid mistakes in the history of the world's most loved sport. It is widely held in soccer circles that France, the favored team, was better than Italy and lost the match largely because of that head-butt, because one player at a pivotal moment let his emotions get the better of him.

The striker who attacked his opponent was the great French player Zinedine Zidane, who ended up—despite the head-butt—being voted the World Cup tournament's most valuable player. Of all the French players, he was the one man the team could least afford to lose. So whom did he attack, and why? The Italian defender was Marco Materazzi, one of the most obnoxious and penalized players in recent soccer history. Materazzi was known to be aggressive and distracting. Throughout the match that day, he had dogged Zidane, hurling vulgarities in his direction. Just prior to the head-butt, video showed Materazzi physically putting his arms around Zidane to prevent him from jumping up as the ball sailed above him. Ultimately, however, it was a vulgar comment from the Italian that caused the attack. The two started back to the opposite end of the field, and Materazzi made a sexual comment about Zidane's sister. That was all Zidane could take apparently, and he responded with the head-butt.

Zidane's momentary angry lapse was a double catastrophe for the French team. Not only did it cost them an outstanding striker as they approached the shootout—Materazzi, by the way, scored a goal for Italy during the shootout, which Italy won 5-3—but it was also an emotional blow to Zidane's teammates, who realized they were facing sudden death at the end of the most important match they would ever play, and their most dependable player had just gotten himself kicked out of the game. It's no great stretch to say France actually lost to Italy the instant Zidane lost his temper. This series of events, naturally, was exactly what Materazzi had been hoping to achieve when he baited his opponent.

This dynamic—attempting to drive an opponent into an intensely emotional state so he or she is distracted and fails to perform up to her or his true ability—is not simply a characteristic of soccer players. We recognize that this phenomenon is often used both in brash and subtle ways by (American) football players, professional poker players, fighters, tennis players, chess grandmasters and many other competitors who want to "get inside the head" of their opponents. That expression, along with "losing one's head," are ways of saying that one competitor has gained an edge by causing an opponent to be absorbed by a particular emotion, like fear or anger, rather than continuing to focus her or his mind on the contest itself.

Seeing how this is an ancient practice, one might ask, "Why does it still work? Why do people still fall for this and let others 'psyche them out'?"

Quite simply it's because **human beings are primarily emotional creatures**. This is not what we assume about ourselves at all—that is, we don't assume that we personally are emotional creatures. We believe we are mostly rational and not emotionally driven. Oh, sure, sometimes we might get a little caught up in what we're feeling at a given moment, but our reasoning and our intellect are usually in charge of all our decisions and actions, right? Often we pride ourselves on just how rational we truly are, especially when we overhear two grownups having a shouting match or see a parent who has lost control of an unruly child in a public place.

No matter what Marco Materazzi might say about *our* sisters, *we* certainly would not have head-butted him because we constantly have our emotions under control. . . . Or do we?

One August afternoon way back in 1977 when I was a chaplain intern at Baylor University Medical Center in Dallas, Texas, I found myself walking through a cancer unit. I had just finished visiting with the family of a patient who was in his last hours. As I went down the hall, I saw a patient aide sobbing profusely. Then I saw a nurse who was weeping. When I got to the nurses' station, I saw a half-dozen administrators and nurses, all of whom were crying. Up and down the unit, I could see people weeping.

Dr. Mike Simpson

What has happened? I wondered. *Has there been some disaster?* As gently as possible, I asked one of the nurses what had happened, why she was crying.

"Oh, haven't you heard?" she said. "Elvis died."

I had to stop and think about that. These hospital staffers all worked on a unit where patients with advanced cancers were treated. Death on that floor was a daily occurrence. All summer I had worked with these professionals and had never seen any sort of expression of sadness. Then they heard that Elvis Presley had died, and all those calloused health care providers were suddenly overcome with genuine grief.

The point is, under the right circumstances any of us can fall prey to powerful emotions. Indeed, Fritz Perls, the father of Gestalt Therapy, once commented that a person has never fully matured until he or she has experienced an explosion of each basic emotion.[i] Most of the time we don't feel overwhelmed by our emotions. Usually we have our feelings under control, so much that we may assume we aren't feeling anything. The reality is, we are always experiencing an emotional state whether we are aware of it or not. *We like to believe we are thinking creatures who have an emotional side. In reality, we are emotional creatures who have the ability to think rationally.* Sometimes.

One really important expression of this distinction—that we are more feeling than thinking creatures—may be seen in that we human beings make very (*very*) few purely logical decisions. *The vast majority of our decisions are based upon emotion rather than reason.* It's only after we decide something that we use our intellectual ability to try to make it seem to ourselves and others that our decisions are based on intellect rather than emotion.

Here is a "thought experiment" that will demonstrate the validity of this observation: 1) Pick a current, extremely controversial, divisive topic—maybe some political or religious issue. 2) Imagine your extended family or a group of co-workers you know well or a gathering of life-long friends all sitting together in one place. 3) Now imagine yourself bringing up that hot-button topic and asking each one of them in turn which side of the issue is correct. Isn't it true that you can predict with almost perfect accuracy where each person will come down on the controversy? Isn't it true that you would know which individuals would likely get into a heated argument with one another over the issue? And isn't it true that, with very few exceptions, no amount of carefully reasoned argument would change anyone's mind? The fanciful quip, "I've already made up my mind; don't confuse me with the facts," is the actual mental state shared by virtually all human beings. If truth be told, the only thing capable of making a purely rational decision based on objectivity and logic is a computer. That will change, of course, when we figure out how to program emotions into computers.

At this point we could digress and discuss the multiple ramifications of the reality that, as humans, we are all much more emotionally than intellectually oriented. For our purposes, however, we simply want to note that, to a greater degree than almost any of us recognize, **human beings are not logically driven, but emotionally driven**. And the more a person insists that she or he is rational rather than emotional, the more that person is emotional chattel because he or she doesn't recognize the sway emotions truly hold over all of us.

Allow me at this point to draw a distinction—one that will help clarify the forces we are describing and also reveal the true power of our emotional states. It's important to recognize there is a difference between what I'm referring to in this section as "emotions" and what most people refer to as "feelings." **Emotions are much deeper, more basic and far more powerful than feelings.** What I mean is, we have two levels of emotions: 1) our "feelings" we are pretty much aware of and our "emotions" that lie deep within us that we are rarely aware of.

To demonstrate what I mean, let's use what I call the *Apple Tree Story*: suppose you are sitting with a group of adults having a significant discussion of some sort, and a child or grandchild of one of the grownups comes into the room. And let's say the child, who is drinking a soda, belches loudly. How would you feel? If you were the parent or grandparent of the child, you might feel *embarrassed*. If you perceived the child to be innocent and innocuous, you might laugh *humorously*. If the discussion were intense or quite significant or if you judged the child to be intentionally trying to draw attention to himself/herself, you might feel *annoyed* or *disgusted*. All these are responses we can call "feelings."

Now let's say this same child is sent outside to play so the grownups can finish their talk. Right outside the room where you are meeting is an apple tree, clearly visible to all the adults through a large window. Everyone sees the child begin to climb the tree without setting down the soda and manage to get to the upper branches. Then suddenly, in the sight of everyone, the child falls and hits the ground and lies without moving. Now every adult in the room is experiencing the very same thing, and it is much stronger and purer—undiluted, so to speak—than whatever each was feeling before. We call this "emotion."

Feelings may be ephemeral, fleeting and "floating on the surface" of our awareness. Emotions are deeper and extremely powerful; often we are not aware we are even experiencing them until they erupt. Feelings may be equated with the "mood of the day," and most grownups can accomplish whatever is necessary regardless of the feelings being experienced. Emotions are profound, underlying states; they are not easily pushed aside (just ask Zinedine Zidane). Every waking, sentient human being is currently dwelling in some emotional state (and you've felt real emotions in your sleep as well, haven't you?). *One key purpose of this book is to help you become aware of yourself as an emotional being.* As we begin discussing our families, let us bear in mind we are and always will be emotional creatures. The people we love and call family are emotional creatures; understanding and working with those emotions will open the door for us to fix our families.

Got to Love Them; After All, They're Family

"Friday, the day after Thanksgiving, is my favorite day of the year." These were the words of a woman in her late 30s spoken as we discussed the stress she was feeling around the upcoming holidays.

"Really?" I said. "Because you do a lot of Christmas shopping on 'Black Friday'?"

"No," she replied shaking her head, "it's because Thanksgiving is my least favorite day of the year, and I'm always so glad when it's over."

This mother of four went on to explain to me that she was her parents' eldest child and the eldest grandchild of her grandparents. About eight or nine years before that conversation, just prior to the birth of her last baby, she had somehow taken over the responsibility for the huge annual four-generation gathering that was her family's Thanksgiving celebration. It was the one occasion when everyone got together. This year, as every year, she knew to expect the same discussions, the same rivalries, the same ruffled feathers and, of course, the same expressions of love. Despite—or maybe because of—knowing what was coming, she was experiencing a great deal of anxiety. Indeed, some mornings she woke up in a near panic, feeling like the sacrificial turkey herself.

"Well," I mused, "why don't you just tell everybody you're not hosting this year?"

A look of absolute horror flashed across her face. "I can't do that! It's my family. It's my responsibility."

Families are awesome and awful, aren't they? *Our families, more than any other force in our lives, have the ability to empower and disempower us—often simultaneously. And what they impart to us, good and ill, can last a lifetime.* When I was kid, every year my father invariably created a reason to embarrass and humiliate me during my mother's family Thanksgiving or Christmas (or both) feast. Usually this was done in the guise of imparting parental wisdom or correction. He desperately wanted to portray himself as a wise, engaged, authoritarian father. "You know, son, the smartest scientists in the world could build a computer as big as this room; and it still wouldn't be able to do everything your brain can do—if only you'd decide to use your brain!"

At the same time, as the oldest grandchild on Mom's side, I had officially been designated as the "family spokesman" by the time I was a teenager. To this day, when I'm with any assortment of my many first cousins on that side and something unusual or challenging is said, they will all look at me, waiting for a response. My job has long been to be the "voice" of my mother's family. Thus, from my childhood, my family was both a source of pain and of power.

Understanding our families and dealing successfully with them to bring about positive change is the primary purpose of this book. It's important, therefore, to be clear when it comes to what I mean when I describe "the family." Do I mean the people who brought you into the world, who theoretically raised you and shared your upbringing: your mother, father, sisters, brothers, steps, halves and blendeds? Yes, to begin with. We will call this your **birth family**. Or do I mean the family you might be most closely related to and live with at this moment, or did for a time, or might in the future: your spouse, partner, children, adoptees, etc.? Yes, that's also what I mean. We'll call these people your **nuclear family**. Do I mean your grandparents, maybe assorted aunts and uncles and maybe some close cousins you grew up with? Yes, of course. We'll call those folks your **family of origin**. Well, what about all those relatives-by-marriage and distant cousins and the excentric uncle people try not to mention; are they family? Sure. They're your **extended family**.[ii]

"Wow," you might say, "those are a whole lot of iterations of what it means to be 'family'!"[iii]

Yes, obviously there is an infinite variety of families from which you can emerge or which you can accumulate. And it's important to recognize how different these families may be from one another and the very different positions you may fill in each.

For instance, if someone asked me whether I come from a small family or a large family, I'd have to say, "Yes and yes." In my birth family—my parents, my sister and I—there were just four of us. Between my two families of origin, however, I'm just one of sixty first cousins. And while, as I indicated, I'm firstborn on my mom's side, on my dad's side I'm right in the middle and there is nothing inherently special about me.

It will pay dividends, even before we get into unpacking the ways you can have a monumental impact in your families, for you to spend some time thinking about the various families to which you belong. Ask yourself what roles you fulfill in each family; what sets each family itself apart to make it special; how does each family compare in terms of ability to cope with life and to offer nurture to those who are part of it?

"Well, wait a minute," you might say. "You've painted the idea of 'family' with a really broad brush. You've included lots of relationships that in times past would not have been considered family at all. This doesn't sound very precise or scientific, as if you're grasping at straws. It makes me wonder if what I heard is true: the concept of "family" in our society has been disintegrating over the last fifty years; the American family and its values are under attack."

This raises an interesting question: is the American family and/or its values really being assaulted, diluted or destroyed? As a professional who has dealt extensively with the family unit, I began to hear in the early 1970s that the whole fabric of the family was under attack. Was that what was really happening? Is that why households seem so disjointed and diverse these days?

Yes, undoubtedly. And also, *no*, not at all.

First, I think it's pretty unlikely that some secret group of powerful people got so sick of old TV programs in the 1950s like *Father Knows Best* and *Leave It to Beaver* that it decided to do anything it could to undermine the American family. Still, it is true that families have changed—largely as a result of our evolving national culture. And these changes have been a real challenge to the conventional framework of the family as portrayed on TV in 1960. The tight, conventional "family" we watched in *Ozzie and Harriet* has morphed into the wildly unconventional group portrayed in *Modern Family*.

It's also worth noting that *a cultural assault on the concept of "family" has been a reality in virtually every society throughout human history*. It's a constant of civilization that every historical expression of family resists the changes that eventually descend upon it. If you think about it, almost every coming-of-age story we read in books or see in the movies deals with young people who—in order to achieve freedom and the ability to express themselves creatively—challenge the values their families imparted to them. Jane Austen's *Pride and Prejudice* is about Elizabeth Bennet's assault on Mr. Darcy's aristocratic family position in pre-Victorian England. The magnificent play *Fiddler on the Roof* deals in large measure with the resilience of the traditional orthodox Jewish family in the face of change in imperial Russia, particularly expressed when Chava, the daughter of the main character Tevye, falls in love with a Christian and marries outside the Jewish community. Another marvelous motion picture that deals with an attack on conventional family values is *Whale Rider*,[iv] in which a Maori chieftain refuses to accept that his mantle of authority can be passed on to a female—a granddaughter—after the death of his grandson and the abdication of his firstborn son. Is the family as we know it under attack? Yes, of course. How else would culture and society evolve? Is it painful? Well, isn't real growth always painful? And beautiful? And ultimately necessary?

In a different—and, for our purposes, more important—way, *the family is not under attack and indeed by definition cannot be undermined or undone.* This is because **human beings invariably and uncannily form themselves into families.** In fact, we don't know how *not* to be family.

Perhaps you've seen one of those internet videos where a group of ducklings or chicks walks single file behind an animal (usually a cat or a dog) that biologically cannot be their parent. When they hatched, these tiny creatures saw not their mother, but this other animal and imprinted on it, treating it from that moment as their mother. These ducklings did not go to Quacker University to learn how to do this. This is an innate behavior to which newborn fowl will invariably adhere.

Ducklings are not the only creatures that have inescapable innate behaviors. Human beings are also born with certain innate behaviors; most interestingly, they come into the world with the ability to feel and express the emotions we've been talking about. And those emotions inexorably draw us into set roles, roles that quickly express themselves as family.

A friend of mine described sitting beside his wife in a birthing center when she was wearing a fetal heart monitor. He noticed his unborn son's heart rate would increase rapidly whenever his wife experienced a contraction. When he asked why this was happening, the attending nurse remarked, "The contraction is frightening the baby."

So children are born with the ability to feel fear. I recall that my own three children as infants could express joy, love and (when they decided Dad was slow in changing their diapers) real anger. They didn't know why they felt a certain way, but their emotions were definitely present.

And it is because human beings all have emotions and we all must deal with those emotions that we automatically form ourselves into families. While it is surely the case we can point to the people who raised us or the people we raised and say, "This is my family," there are also other groups with whom we form family bonds. *Every human family is a creation of its members' response to shared emotional experiences.* We could go so far as to say that what truly makes us "family" is not that we are biologically or legally yoked to others, but that we have shared the most profound emotional experiences with them. Typically it is our biological family with whom we have experienced those emotions, but it can also be the case that there are other groups to which we belong that are family to us as well.

Now that's a pretty brash claim, very far-reaching. Let me break it down a little with another thought experiment: the *Elevator Story*. Suppose you and six total strangers got stuck between floors in an elevator and it took the fire department two hours to get you out. By the end of that 120 minutes when the elevator started rolling again and the doors opened, you seven would have formed yourselves into a family. At least one of you would have emerged as a leader. One would likely have become an annoyance to a greater or lesser degree. The calmer, more nurturing ones would be comforting the stressed-out ones. Of course, these are exactly the roles your biological/legal family members would automatically fall into if they were the ones trapped in the elevator with you. In fact, you already know who in your family would fall into which role.

Follow the logical progression of this notion and it becomes clear that we are constantly forming ourselves into little families: your bridge group or bowling team is a family; the members of your house of worship are a family; the people you work with are a family, as are the other students in your exercise class. The reality is that your informal family bonds can be extraordinarily powerful and controlling, just slightly less so than those of your "real" family.[v]

In the hyper-realistic World War II movie *Saving Private Ryan*, a soldier is intentionally sought out to be sent home from France to the United States because all three of his brothers have been killed in combat. The initial reaction of the soldier upon hearing this is to refuse to leave the front: "Then I'm going to stay here—with the only brothers I have left."

We might think that the life-or-death experiences of military combat were what deepened the soldier's bonds to such profound levels. Isn't it true, however, that similar loyalty is also present among groups of such ultimate insignificance as avid fans of sports teams, to the extent that they will insult and denigrate supporters of opposing sports teams—people exactly like them in every way—just for wearing the "wrong color"?

I once attended the funeral of a fine, generous man who was buried wearing a bright orange jacket and purple pants. At the end of the service, the "Tiger Rag" fight song was played. All of this was meant to be the final, parting affirmation of his allegiance to Clemson University. In our lucid, unemotional moments, we would all admit that emotional loyalty of this depth is really over the top, that no one institution is more deserving than another of this abiding affection . . . unless of course you're a former student of the University of North Texas, in which case pride and loyalty make perfect sense (you do get my jokes, don't you?). So, yes, unofficial, informal family bonds can be ephemeral. Or they can be as powerful and enduring as the bonds that yoke us to our biological families. *Whatever experiences bind us together in a shared emotional network are actually turning us into families.*

My friend Dennis Lundblad came up with an excellent way to describe the emotional network that binds us together into our various families. He calls it the **river of emotion**. For several reasons, I've always found this to be a very appropriate metaphor.

For instance, a river can change and be very different from one season to another, from one day to the next. Sometimes the river is high and smooth; sometimes it overflows its banks; sometimes it slows to little more than a trickle; and sometimes it gets all jammed up with debris that prevents anything from floating downstream (we're going to come back to that idea shortly). The same is true for the emotional networks we share with our families. Often, most of the people in a close family network are sharing the same emotion at the same time.

This is certainly true when there are big events that strike everyone in the family: if there is a death of a cherished family member, everyone feels grief; if there is a long-anticipated wedding, there is shared joy; if there is great uncertainty about the welfare of a family member, everyone is quite anxious. Have you ever paid attention to the reality that most of your family members share a common emotional state at any given time? Ever see that refrigerator magnet that reads, "When Momma ain't happy, ain't nobody happy"? Isn't it true that one or two individuals set the emotional tone for each of your families, and everyone else in the family seems to know what they *should be* feeling?

Another reason I like the emotional river as a metaphor is that a river implies immersion in a common, shared emotional stream in which all humanity is included. We are all floating in the river of emotion, and we cannot escape the river. There is a part of us that naturally wants to resist the notion that we are irrevocably caught up in this emotional dimension we've described. We want to believe we can opt out of being emotionally driven people and not be a part of a reality we share with all those folks who irritate us. Well, sorry. You're in the river, and you're saturated with all the different types of emotions and feelings there are, like everybody else. And it is the inescapable nature of this river of emotion to draw us together. As we bob about in the river, we reach out to the others about us to help us find support in the face of the river's changeable current.

While nobody and nothing—including this book—can transport you out of the river, we can do the next best thing. We can learn how to make this river your servant rather than continuing to allow yourself to bob helplessly downstream.

I also like the river of emotion as a metaphor because rivers are living things and they are going somewhere. Unlike a pond or a lake or a swamp, a river isn't sedentary.[vi] Every drop of water in a river was in some sense created as a new beginning, as a raindrop or snow melt or glacial aquifer or a mountain spring, and it's going somewhere. It has been claimed by the river to be a part of a journey. Rivers have always been highways. The great inland cities of the world virtually all began alongside rivers. This implies something about our river of shared emotions: it is taking us somewhere. Together with the others in our families, our emotions are taking us on a shared journey. If it feels that your family has gotten "dammed up" and isn't making any real progress (or even any movement in any direction) on your voyage, then you are reading the right book.

Shouldn't We Be Moving?

Something was wrong with Hank.[vii] All the board members of the small non-profit I ran were excited about Hank finally taking on the role of Board Chair, which he did on a January 1st. The problem was that the cooperative, optimistic, enthusiastic Hank who had been a volunteer for so long was no longer the fellow we

Dr. Mike Simpson

inherited as our top elected leader. Hank suddenly seemed to want to second-guess everything we did. He tended to pour cold water on any bright, new idea that the staff presented, so that expanding our outreach program became a real chore. While the chair was supposed to conduct our monthly board meetings, to make sure they kept flowing and to end the meetings in about an hour, Hank began to offer soliloquies after each individual report—long diatribes that became increasingly dour and pessimistic and resulted in meetings that dragged on interminably.

In late summer, when the time came to plan our annual holiday fund-raising feast, Hank announced he was in favor of shutting the whole event down. While I knew we could probably override his wishes and hold the festival anyway, I didn't want there to be an open conflict and a divisive struggle on the board that would certainly put someone in the position of being a loser. Plus I was concerned about what was going on with my friend Hank. Thus I decided to ask him if we could have lunch together and spend an hour discussing the holiday festival.

As soon as we ordered our meals at the little sandwich shop, before he could say anything, I inquired about his son, Jerry. Had Jerry, who was a tech whiz, gotten a fulltime job with a computer outfit yet? Hank gave me a blank look. Clearly the question had surprised him. He spent about ten minutes telling me how Jerry had pretty much frittered away all the money he made from his last contract job with a digital design company. Hank's young twenty-something son apparently laid around all day in his apartment, playing internet video games and chatting online with people he had met through social media. As far as Hank could see, Jerry was wasting his life. Beyond that, Jerry seemed to be completely withdrawn; and Hank thought he was a little depressed.

When he was winding up his comments regarding his son, I quickly interjected, "How about Lydia? I guess I heard she didn't move home at the end of the spring semester." Once again, Hank was totally surprised. His daughter, Lydia, was a brilliant student who graduated near the top of her high-school class and captured a partial scholarship to a prestigious university. At the end of a lackluster freshman year, instead of coming home for the summer, she remained seventy-five miles away, living with a young man— not a fellow student, but a seemingly ne'er-do-well fellow with no evident source of income. After meeting the boyfriend and spending a few minutes around him (all the time they could bear), Hank and his wife Brenda decided this youth's job was selling drugs and that Lydia was not only his live-in servant, but his client as well. Tears beginning to well in his eyes, Hank said, "Brenda and I just aren't sure what we should do. This isn't like our daughter at all."

"Yes," I agreed. "This must be terribly distressing for the two of you, especially with Brenda's medical problem."

A jolt ran through Hank. Then he shook his head in frustration. "The doctors still haven't been able to say for sure what is causing the loss of feeling in her hands." For several months, Brenda had been suffering with spreading neuropathy in her fingers. An accomplished pianist, Brenda had to stop playing. As the condition progressed, it was becoming clear she would eventually lose her ability to drive and feed herself. In an effort to diagnose the source of her loss of feeling, she had been subjected to tests on her neck and her arms, nerves and muscles. Hank explained that one neurosurgeon wanted to perform experimental surgery on her spine, arguing that the source of her problem had to be pressure on her nerves, even if it didn't show up in MRI scans.

"This is an awful lot for you to bear, Hank," I said, "especially with your new job. How's that going, by the way?"

He just shrugged. "It's a job. Nothing especially good or bad about it."

A few weeks prior to becoming our board chair—and before any of the cascade of misfortune in his family had begun—Hank had been the victim of a holiday lay-off. After devoting more than thirty years to a regional company and rising to the position of comptroller, he lost his job when his firm was acquired by a larger, national corporation. Hank's entire division was judged to be redundant, and all in it were laid off. After toying with the idea of early retirement for a month or so, he had utilized an employment agency and found work as an accountant with a small tax firm.

"You know, Hank," I said in reflection, "it is almost as if your whole family is 'snake bit.' And the worst of it is you never had a chance to get over the way you were mistreated and lost your *whole career after all those years of loyalty."*

It seemed to me that a brief look of awareness flashed across his face. "Well . . . my new job, it's not so bad. I don't have to answer to a board of directors—like you do—and it's simple stuff. I get to help a lot of people."

I glanced at my watch. "Looks like I used up all our time without getting to the real reason I wanted to have lunch. What do you think we need to change so you can live with the Holiday Festival?"

"Oh that. Have you got people to run it? Is the funding in place?"

"Sure," I replied. "Generally we net three or four thousand more than our expenses."

"Yeah. I knew that. No, I guess I don't have any problem with the festival. Let's go forward with it."

As ponderously long as it is, this example of Hank and his family is well-suited for our purposes at this point in several ways. First of all, it worked—and I *don't* mean it worked because it was a subtle way of getting Hank to drop his resistance to the Holiday Festival. It worked because it enabled Hank to focus on the real issues in his life and recognize our organization was not the problem he kept trying to turn it into. It also worked because, following this lunch, Hank's family problems uncannily began to atrophy. Brenda's neuropathy began to reverse itself, and she eventually recovered her ability to play the piano, loudly. Lydia's boyfriend called her from jail one night, asking her to use some of her leftover college fund to bail him out and to hire a lawyer. She hung up on him. The next day she moved back to her parents' home and began the process of becoming a volunteer for AmeriCorps. Computer whiz Jerry landed an IT job that required him to relocate to a large, east-coast metro area. Within a few weeks, he was the head of the tech department. The tax accountant who hired Hank was so impressed with his work that he asked him to become a partner in the firm. Hank declined, saying he and Brenda had long dreamed of travel and the added responsibility of partnership would interfere with the excursions they were planning (though facts and circumstances have been altered, all this is true.).

It's also well-suited in that it reveals quite clearly the extent of the network, the emotional river, flowing through a family. In terms of the "emotional process," Hank had never recovered from the grief and anger of being laid off, something he assumed would never happen to a person as loyal and competent as himself. The ripples of his despair spread through his nuclear family, each person dealing with it uniquely. It might seem that each person was overreacting. My observation would be that these were actually not catastrophic overreactions but fairly typical for a major disruption in the family.

This example is also well-suited for our discussion because *it presents a different paradigm for understanding family problems and a different outlook concerning how to deal with them.* Suppose, in accord with our conventional medical and psychological models, a family with similar problems came to the attention of a counselor or a physician. The daughter, Lydia, might have been placed in a drug treatment program. The son, Jerry, might have been diagnosed as depressed or ADHD and put on medication. The wife, Brenda, probably would have endured thousands of dollars' worth of various medical tests and neurological treatments and ultimately been told her problem was psychosomatic and she needed counseling. Clearly any of these three could have been seen as the "identified patient," that is, the "sick" or "troubled" person in the family who needed diagnosis and treatment. The alternative *Fix Your Family* way of looking at this is to say that the real pathology was in the family itself and that it actually originated in the one who seemed the least troubled of all—Hank, the husband and father.

Another reason this example works is because it demonstrates several of the precepts of the **Emotional Process** theory that we use in this text to deal with family issues. An essential truth we can see at work in Hank's family is *healing is a natural process*. We have no trouble recognizing the truth of this if we're talking about a physical ailment or an injury. When I was fourteen and suffered a broken collarbone, the orthopedic surgeon didn't have to send my clavicle to group therapy or give it sedatives. He seemed to sense that the bones would intuitively know how to heal. Yet, when it comes to emotional issues in individuals and families, we as a society seem to perceive that a burdened mind cannot possibly mend. We believe it will perpetually need drugs and\or therapy. In life, natural healing happens all the time. When a loved one dies, we grieve for a period of time, and then we are able to resume leading a normal life again. This is not to say that traumatic events disappear from our psyche. We may have "gotten over" them, but we will long remember the attacks of Pearl Harbor and of 911, just as I can still predict the weather, courtesy of my long-healed collarbone.

If healing is a natural process, we might ask then, why is it so many people—and families—don't seem to get well? The insight of the Emotional Process model is that, *when healing doesn't naturally occur, something is impeding the healing process*. This is certainly true with physical healing. If you think about it, virtually all medical intervention, from antibiotics to chemo, is not actually meant to heal us; rather, medical treatment is intended to attack those things—bacteria, fever, cancer cells, inflammation—that prevent the natural process of our bodies from getting well. Medicine is not to make us well but to overcome those things that prevent us from healing. The principle holds true with the personal and familial issues we face.

In Hank's case, it was his unmitigated despair that interrupted his family's ability to proceed successfully in their journeys. In reflecting on the example of Hank and his family, you might ask, "Well, why did you go to the trouble of having lunch and bringing up all that family stuff? Why didn't you just point out to him that he had never gotten over the grief of being laid off and that it was causing a lot of trouble for everyone in his family?"

That would be a correct *rational* response, pretty much guaranteed to fail. Telling someone what their issues are is an intellectual process. For Hank to grasp what was happening, he had to experience the full emotional process, to be reminded of the various emotional states he had been dealing with for months.

There are, to be sure, a great variety of ways to help people encounter and work through the emotional issues that have inhibited their emotional well-being and interfered with their families and relationships. **The purpose of this book is to help you understand your families, to see what is inhibiting their well-being and, where possible, to move them toward emotional healing**.

That brings us to the last insight we'll share in this first chapter. The conventional way to view family issues is to hang a diagnosis on someone. We often hear comments like, "Jerry's bipolar behavior has caused everyone in the family to be stressed out. His mom became so troubled by the drama, she had an episode and had to be medicated. His sister won't even talk to him anymore. I'm afraid they've become permanently estranged."

Rather than diagnosing your family with any of the prevailing psychological, medical or reality-TV descriptions, I'd like to encourage you to use a different, technical term that can pretty much apply to any pervasive family problem: **stuck**. Hank's family was stuck. Stuckness pervaded the entire nuclear family. When Hank got "unstuck," the whole family was able to move on.[viii]

Remember the term "river of emotion"? It's particularly helpful here. Logjams can occur in any river and especially in the emotional rivers in which we find ourselves. We want to be able to remove these emotional logjams so that our families can get unstuck and see what happens as they flow on down the river.

The next step we must take in this process is to discover where and how our families got stuck in the first place.

Key Ideas set forth in Chapter One:
- Human beings are primarily emotional creatures; we universally underestimate the degree to which we are emotionally driven.
- Human beings invariably and uncannily form themselves into families, not just biologically and legally, but primarily through shared emotional experiences.
- Understanding and dealing successfully with our families, including bringing about needed change, will be the primary focus of this book.
- In all of our families, we are connected to others and continually immersed in a river of shared emotion; the study and utilization of this river of emotion is called "Emotional Process."
- With emotional issues, just as with physical ailments, healing is a natural process.

- Rather than resorting to multiple diagnoses, healers and treatments, in this text we will refer to the issues that trouble individuals and families as "stuckness"; our intention is to learn how to get unstuck.

2
Your Family: Booby Traps or Buried Treasure?

Of course, you know what a *parable* is, right? Here's a really short, really famous parable that has the potential to help you perceive your family in a new light:

The kingdom of heaven is like treasure hidden in a field which someone found and hid, then in his joy he goes and sells all that he has and buys that field. —Mt. 13:44

Like other biblical parables attributed to Jesus of Nazareth, the story of "Treasure Buried in a Field" has certain predictable characteristics: it's short, simple, has only a few characters, is culturally rooted and has a twist in it that is designed to provoke deep reflection. Like all true parables regardless of their origin (Jesus wasn't the only one to use parables), the ultimate purpose of this kind of literature is to take our assumptions about the world and turn them upside down.[ix]

Since parables are meant to challenge our way of thinking, what's the unusual aspect of this particular parable that causes us to see reality in a new way? I think most of us would say it's the "winning the lottery" moment: a fellow is going about the mundane, repetitive tasks he has endured every day for years, then stumbles onto something that instantly, totally changes his existence in one fell swoop. Seems like that the point of the story.

Or maybe not. I mean, isn't it the case that everybody has fantasized about a sudden windfall that lifts us above the financial hardship and drudgery of ordinary life? What's so special about a story in which that happens? And it's pretty clear that Jesus never equated wealth with godliness. So what else should we be noticing about this parable?

Maybe asking the *right questions* will help open up this parable in a little different way. So here is one possibility: why did the man buy the field? Why did he need the field? I mean, once he had the treasure, the field was extraneous. Why not just take the treasure, hide it in some secure place that only he knew about and forget about farming forever? Now we could argue at length about the nuances of the story, about Palestinian property rights and about the availability of safe-deposit boxes in the first century, but I'd like to offer an alternative explanation that just might shine a different light on this man's actions.

Those who first heard this parable would assume the main (okay, the only) character in the parable was a farmer who was working a plot of land he rented from someone else. This was a common first century practice and, we noted, parables are culturally rooted. He paid his rent with crops he raised and sold. And let's say the farmer—let's call him Isaac—had worked this field for years. While it was ordinary in its fertility, it was difficult for Isaac to work. It was physically hard to get to and, more than that, the soil was full of rocks. Over the years he had perfected the art of plowing deep enough to plant his crops, but not so deep as to hit the numerous stones beneath the surface. One morning, however, perhaps because his ox pulled more quickly than he expected or because he forced down on the plow's handle a little too firmly, the blade of the plow struck a rock and lodged there. Isaac couldn't pull the plow loose. Angrily, probably afraid the blade was bent or broken, he untied the ox and got down on his hands and knees to work the plow free. It was as he pulled away handfuls of dirt that he saw the obstacle was not a rock, but rather some sort of small, wooden chest. The blade of the plow had broken it open, and he saw the glint of gold and the shimmer of fine jewels. It was a treasure intentionally buried in this inauspicious plot of land. Isaac, after he caught his breath, decided to unearth the chest, tie the treasure to his ox and take it home. As he thought about how best to proceed—after all, suddenly becoming very wealthy does change one's life—he stopped. He got to his feet and gazed around the dusty field. This ground, he remembered, was full of rocks. . . . What if those weren't rocks? What if they were lots more treasure chests? Isaac smiled as he decided, "I have to buy this field."

"Well, okay," you might say, "so the farmer decided to buy the field because there wasn't one but a whole multitude of treasures buried in it. That's interesting, I suppose. Hadn't thought of it. But what exactly does it have to do with me and my family?"

I'm suggesting that your family is like that farmer's field. If your family were a plot of ground and we assumed that family problems were "rocks," just how "rocky" would it be? Again, if you're reading this for any reason other than idle curiosity or a course assignment, the chances are your family is a rocky pasture indeed. Suppose, however, that all those obstacles that have been booby-traps in the past—the taboo subjects, the hostile conflicts, the broken relationships—were actually capable of being transformed into riches, into empowering, liberating treasures? Going forward, that's exactly what we're up to: turning your family's emotional brokenness into emotional riches. And, since you're already part-owner of the farm, all it will take is a little digging on your part.

Picture Your Family

If you're going to dig up a field full of treasure, the first thing you'll need is a shovel. To excavate the treasure hidden in your family, on the other hand, the first tool you'll need is a blank paper and a pencil. We'll going to draw a **family gram**.[x]

So you'll know where we're going with this, below is a family gram of Hank Tyler and his family, whose story you read at the end of Chapter One.

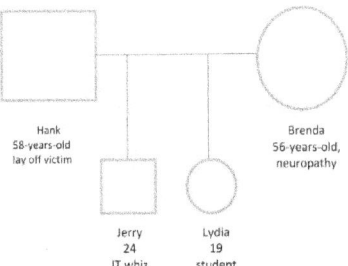

And below are the basic symbols. While there are some common conventions used in making these drawings, there are no hard-and-fast rules about how to proceed. Just use the guidelines we are providing here as a way of knowing what questions to ask, what information to seek and what may be helpful as you study your family gram. At the end of this chapter, we will present a fully-developed family gram; then, in Chapter Three, we will unlock

Dr. Mike Simpson

some of the treasure you may find hidden in your family's diagram.

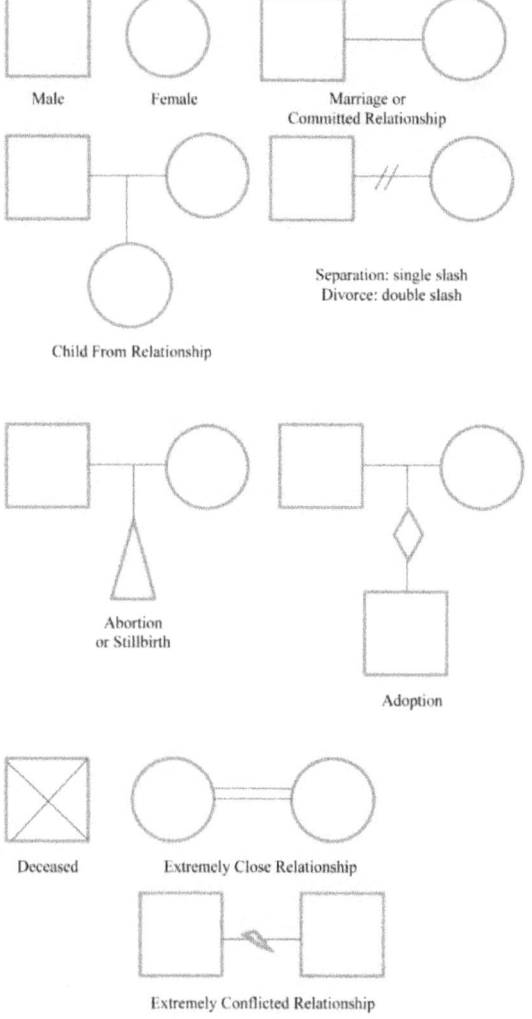

Let's illustrate a slightly more complicated family, the Donaldson family, with the inclusion of four generations. This diagram demonstrates how preceding and succeeding generations are included in the family gram. It also gives us the opportunity to see relationships that are very close, conflicted and estranged, as illustrated by the diagram below.

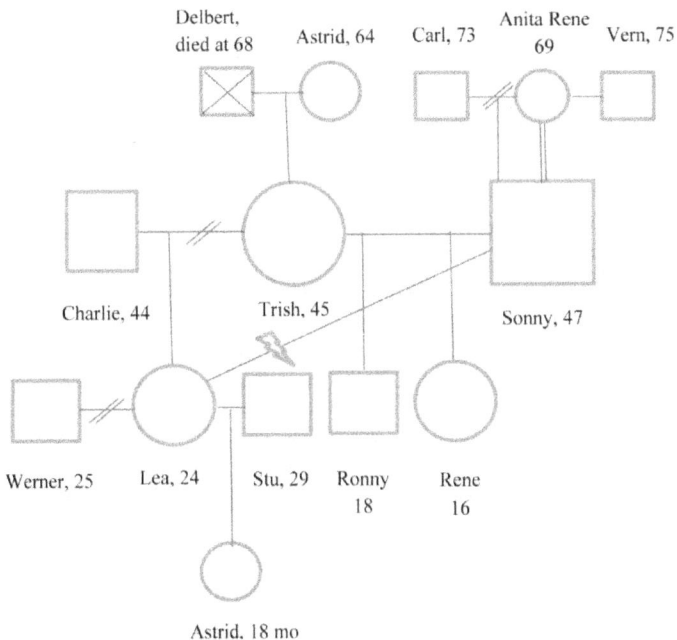

Donaldson family description: to understand the significance of a family gram, it helps to focus on one individual and move from that person to understand the relationships and history of the entire family constellation. With the Donaldson family, you might look first at *Lea* on the third row, second from the left; note that she is twenty-four, was married to *Werner* and, after leaving him, married *Stu*, with whom she has an eighteen-month-old daughter, *Astrid*. Lea herself is the child of a divorced couple; her mother *Trish* was married to *Charlie*; after Lea's birth, she left Charlie and married *Sonny*, with whom she had Lea's half-brother and sister, *Ronny* and *Rene*. Note that Lea doesn't get along well with her stepfather Sonny. The family gram also illustrates Lea's grandparent generation: Trish's parents are *Delbert*, who is deceased, and *Astrid*; Sonny's birthparents are *Carl* and *Anita Rene*, who divorced after Sonny's birth and Anita Rene married

Vern. While Sonny has a rocky relationship with Lea, note that he is close to his mother. Most hand-drawn family grams contain a lot more information than what is contained on this diagram, which we've kept pretty simple (mostly because it looks a lot cleaner). Also, this diagram illustrates the "current ages" of family members; we observe that your family gram will be more accurate and workable if you list birth years rather than current ages (the Donaldson family is lucky; they'll never get any older).

When drawing a family gram, you may find it helpful to begin in the middle of the page and try to leave space above and below whichever generation of your family you start with. As you draw symbols for family members, try to list as much of the following information as you can learn: names (full names and nicknames are often surprisingly important), birthdates, death dates, marriage dates, occupations, other significant factors that might impact the family (diseases, credentials, achievements, tragic events, and so forth). Try to write down whatever the family would find most significant.

As you construct the family gram, be particularly watchful of relationships. To whom is an individual especially close? From whom is a person emotionally cut-off? As you look at these relationships, you'll want to ask yourself what impact these various relationships have had on the family as a whole. If Mom and Dad had an off-again/on-again relationship, how did the rest of the family deal with it?

Look for events and characteristics that repeat in succeeding generations. These patterns can have a huge impact on the direction of your family. One fellow who was working on his family gram remarked to me, "I recall angrily yelling at my two sons, ages 6 and 4, over some truly minor irritant. As I walked away from them, I asked myself, 'Now why did I jump on the boys like that? Oh yeah, that's the way my dad used to correct me.'" We will talk more about the astonishing extent to which the *past formats the future.*

As you build your family gram, it will help you to be aware of the extent to which you are aware or unaware of the life history of preceding generations. If you find there are large blank areas—for instance, you don't know your grandmother's maiden name, where your parents were born, how many cousins you have—a good question to ask is, why didn't this information get passed along to me? Was it considered unimportant or were facts even intentionally concealed? Do the blank areas relate to significant, unspoken realities in my family's history?

I recall being in my late 30s when it dawned on me that I had never heard my father mention his deceased brother Leslie—even though my sister was named for him. And then it occurred to me that everything I knew about my father's family relationships had been related to me by my mother. Dad had never spoken to me about his family at all beyond an occasional anecdote from his childhood. I realized immediately this was something I needed to address with my dad. We'll discuss some of the process and results of this in Chapter Five when we talk about "love bombs."

Finding these "missing pieces" of information is the next step in working on your family gram. Make a list of what you don't know and ask yourself who can fill in the blanks. You will learn that sleuthing out the missing information from the past is going to cast new, revealing light on your family, even to the point of changing some assumptions and beliefs you've had for a lifetime. As I said about my dad's family, my mom told me all I knew about them until I began to investigate. I learned that many things Mom told me were mistaken.

There are certain significant topics to discuss during your work on your family gram. These will be the focus of the following section. As we proceed to list and discuss these, let me first encourage you to be as honest as possible in describing your family through the diagram. To paraphrase the great therapist Virginia Satir, "If somebody is unzipped, he's unzipped!" If a relationship is conflicted and you gloss over that in your family gram, not only will you be unable to deal with any pertinent issue, you won't even have a clear idea of what the real issue is.

Digging Around in Your Family Plots

There is an amazing tree growing in the historical cemetery in Colonial Williamsburg, Virginia. It's called "the Mother-in Law Tree." As the story goes, in the 1680s a woman named Mrs. Harrison, an aristocratic matriarch, had a distinct distaste for her son-in-law, James Blair, and did everything within her power to come between him and her daughter Sarah. Eventually they all died (funny how that keeps happening) and were buried in the great family plot behind the church. Some years later, a sycamore tree sprouted and eventually shaded the entire plot. The above-ground roots of the tree grew between the headstones, literally forcing the husband and wife apart and moving the daughter's marker to within a few inches of her mother.

Have you ever experienced that kind of animosity? Let's hope at least we can make some changes so such broken relationships don't extend to the grave—and even beyond.

Now we get to talk about how your family members relate to one another. Obviously, relationships change over the lifetimes of those in them. With the tools you can gain from *Fix Your Family*, our intention is that you can have a great deal of sway over how well many of the relationships in your family work. At this point we're not going to talk about relating in a "healthy," workable, highly-functional manner. That comes later. Chances are you already know what an unhealthy, negative relationship is like: it feels bad and it's some variation and combination of painful, frustrating, frightening, anxiety-producing and usually in some way irrevocably repetitive (that sounds like a good definition of stuckness). Being specific about why a relationship doesn't work is an important step in changing it, even if you don't like the idea of examining broken relationships too closely.

Let's take a look at some characteristics of relationships. We'll use two hypothetical tools to assist us here: the **distance scale** and the **conflict scale**. Please note that these are not diagnostic tools, but rather descriptive categories. The intention of placing your family on either of these scales is to help you obtain a clear, sharply-focused understanding of how members of your family relate to one another. Remember: when it comes to how families relate, there is no golden standard of "normal" or "ideal" you're trying to attain. Each family is unique. Therefore, it will have its own unique pathology and its own unique expression of well-being.[xi]

Regarding the distance scale, when it comes to *emotional distance*, does your family as a whole tend to be close or distant? You've seen family relationships in which those involved seem to be a little too close: husbands and wives who don't go to the restroom without checking in with their spouses; children who have never lived at any geographical distance—and frankly do not have emotional permission to do so—from their parents; dependent individuals who are not able to voice any opinion that differs from those other individuals who dominate their lives. We'll call relationships characterized by such impenetrable closeness **fused** or **bound**. Is anyone in your family emotionally fused to another family member? While we may recognize what they are giving up by being "joined at the hip," another good question is, what do they gain by maintaining such closeness?

"Why does Uncle Marvin always go along with what Aunt Wilma says? Doesn't he have a mind of his own? Have they always been fused like that? Do they really like it?"

Then there is the opposite extreme: the emotionally **estranged** or **cut-off** relationship. Maybe you've had the experience of someone abruptly leaving a family gathering when a particular individual showed up unexpectedly, or maybe someone turned and walked away just at the mention of the detested person's name. Often it's not so obvious, but still an observable reality: emotionally-distant family members will greet the person they dislike and have two minutes of pained conversation while everyone around them, on pins-and-needles, tries not to appear interested in their encounter.

One reality often expressed by those who work with Emotional Process is *cut-offs do not heal*. To say it another way, *estrangement is not a cure for any family ill*. Rather it is a sort of cryogenic freezing of disharmony. Whatever the issue might be, it will remain in the deep freeze until the next family gathering where it can be trotted out, danced around and quickly put back in the family's cold storage.

As you think about any estrangement in your family, you might ask yourself, what is the real reason these people have decided to invest so much energy in mutual, smoldering hatred? Funny how the expressed friction is almost never the real source of dispute. Acknowledging the real issue might make them both look silly and immature. On the other hand, if you have a sense of what the real problem is, you have taken the first step toward healing that relationship, as you will see.

Now let's consider the other scale: *conflict*. How do members of your family handle disputes? Is there a lot of discord, or are problems glossed over and basically ignored to the greatest extent possible? At one extreme of this scale are relationships that exist in constant, **chronic conflict**. People, often husbands and wives, relate to one another with animosity, hostility and rage that is amazing predictable in its regularity. One wonders how such individuals come together in the first place. Did each person have a personal "script" that caused him/her to accept on the deepest, inner level that they were not supposed to live in a happy, mutual, intimate relationship, but rather that their life together should be constantly moving toward another vitriolic argument?

The epitome of this might be found in the example of the actor Humphrey Bogart, who was married four times to four beautiful, very strong-willed, temperamental actresses. His third marriage, that lasted from 1938 through 1945, was to Mayo Methot. There was so much conflict, including physical violence, that the Hollywood press dubbed the couple "The Battling Bogarts." For his part—at least until he met and fell for Lauren Bacall anyway—Bogart seemed content with the drama and discord, allegedly saying, "I wouldn't give you two cents for a dame without a temper."

At the far end of the spectrum from those who are perpetually in conflict are those who never seem to fight at all. Some theorists call these folks **super reasonable**. One is tempted to think that such folks live in a constant state of harmony. To be sure, there are serene individuals out there in the world. It's more likely, however, that the "conflict avoidance" folks in your family are actually emotionally inhibited or, as it is said, they "stuff their feelings." In families where there seems to be no conflict, you might encounter mysterious, unyielding physical or psychological health issues (remember Hank's wife, Brenda, who unaccountably lost feeling in her fingers). There are also many other ways in which members of avoidance families "act out": unexpected legal problems; sudden "morality" issues; dramatic, unpredictable developments that change the family makeup (such as Hank's daughter, Lydia, moving in with a drug dealer).

As you place your family on these two theoretical scales, you might think of other families with which you are familiar. What is the most emotionally fused family you know? The most emotionally estranged? Do you know a family whose members fight constantly? What about a family that never fights—and does disharmony show itself within that family in other ways? While, again, these scales are neither diagnostic nor indicative of ideal, normal relationships, it's probably the case that families who tend to dwell at the extremes of the scales do not function as well, are not as resilient in the face of new challenges and aren't as much fun to be part of as families that are less extreme on the distance and conflict scales. It's also worth noting that families can change how they relate, that no family is perpetually constrained to remain at one spot on either scale.

The Right Questions and How to Ask Them

Using the distance and conflict scales doesn't require much interaction with your family. All you have to do is reflect on your own past experience and observations. As you move forward in fleshing out your family grams, however, you'll need a special tool to aid your actual interactions with your family members. That marvelous tool, one that you will perceive as growing in importance throughout your investigation as you refine your ability to use it, is **asking questions**.

Doesn't that sounds simplistic and stupid? On the other hand, did you know you can say things using questions rather than making statements? Were you aware that questions tend to move us "out of our emotions and into our thoughts"? And what do you think about the fact that this paragraph is made up entirely of questions?

Now that you have begun a diagram of your family, and now that you have evaluated how emotionally close they are and how conflict is expressed and dealt with in their relationships, it's time to figure out just how your family got to where it is. For that, you'll need to ask questions. Asking the right question in the right manner can unleash tremendous learning and new awarenesses as well as some powerful emotions within you as the questioner, and certainly within those you are asking (as an aside here, let's note that we will be lingering on how best to present yourself and interact with family members in Chapter Four).

Josh Wilson, a Christian minister, sat beside his father Dan at the kitchen table of his Aunt Velma. Josh had explained to his father a few weeks before that he was on a "family tour" to

Dr. Mike Simpson

deepen his knowledge of the extended clan of which he was a part, but with which he was not well-acquainted. Dan was quite impressed by Josh's family gram, which caused him to recognize there were things about his family he also didn't know, Dan suggested that he accompany Josh as he visited some of their kinfolks. As the youngest of seven children, Dan was particularly interested in visiting some of his aging siblings whom he hadn't seen in several years.

Aunt Velma, Dan's oldest sister, responded enthusiastically as she listened to Josh explain his project. She helped him check the accuracy of his family gram. Getting into the spirit of the quest, Velma went to her bedroom closet and returned with a box of old photos.

As she shuffled through the pictures, she said ruefully, "I don't think I have one of Grandma Agatha. She didn't let people take her photo. Did you know Grandma, Dan?"

"She died before I was born. Didn't she live down in Saint Louis?"

"Yes. Our dad quit taking us across the river after she died. He said there was no reason to go." Absently she said, "And when we went to see her, we had to get to her house before dark on Friday."

Josh's ears perked up. "Before sundown Friday? Why was that?"

Velma went on to describe Grandma's strict weekend schedule, her eating habits and the rigorous dress code that applied to the women who visited her.

"Aunt Velma," Josh asked, "what was your grandmother's maiden name?"

Velma had to stop and think. "Gold, I think. No, it was Goldberg."

Josh sat silently contemplating this new discovery. He turned to his father and began, "Dad, did you know—"

"No," his father said with an expression of wonder. "I had no idea we were Jewish."

All sorts of surprises—some awesome and delightful, some eerie and ironic—are in store for you as you continue investigating your family gram. Whether you really appreciate what you learn or you cringe and wish you hadn't started the project (and I warn you that you'll have both positive and negative experiences), I would like to make several predictions about the ultimate outcome of your work: 1) you'll gain a sense of awareness and empowerment unlike anything you've experienced before; 2) you'll see your family in a new, appreciative light; 3) you'll become a different kind of authority and leader within your family; 4) you'll encounter unanswered questions about your family that will intrigue you and compel you to dig deeper into your "field of treasures"; and 5) you'll become quite adroit at the use of questions to discover those things you want to know.

Using questions to further your search for information about your family is a nuanced topic on which we could spend lots of time. For our purposes here, however, are a few pertinent observations about questions.

We should note that *there are at least three ways to ask any one question*, and your ability to ask a question in the most productive way will be an enormous help in getting the information you're after. Here is a thought experiment that may help demonstrate this:

Let's suppose you had a great aunt, Lois, who died suddenly at a relatively young age; she was forty-nine and fell off a trolley car while riding up a hill during a vacation in San Francisco (yes, yes, a farfetched example). Lois has three grown children, none of whom has shown any inclination to discuss Lois, her life history or her untimely and somewhat absurd death. You want to discuss certain elements of her life history, but you realize that to get there, you're going to have to deal with the forbidden topic of her fatal accident.

As you sit with Valerie, the eldest child and only daughter, you casually bring her mother into the conversation. Valerie begins to cry. From your past experiences with her, you know that Valerie is extremely emotional, always expressing her feelings quite openly. So you say, "Gosh, Val, you are still so sad about your mom's passing, aren't you?" At that, Valerie begins to sob and talk about her mom. As you listen to the outpouring, you quietly wait for the opportunity to ask for the specific information you desire.

The middle child—Arthur we'll call him—is a sort of buttoned-down guy who is the opposite of Valerie in that he never expresses any emotion. As you did with his sister, you sit talking about extraneous matters, then begin to describe your own last interaction with Lois. Though his expression scarcely changes, you can't help but notice the tears beginning to form at the corners of his eyes and trace down his cheeks. "Arthur," you say in a curious tone, "do you know you're crying?" He responds, as you might expect, by touching his face to verify the truth of your observation. Then he thinks about it for a moment and says, "I guess I still miss Mom more than I realized." Then, making sure to linger on his thoughts and not his emotional state, you calmly begin to ask him some factual questions about Lois.

Then there is the baby of the family, Luther. Let's say he's a scamp who craves attention and always manages to make himself the focus of any gathering—regardless of the reason for the get-together. As you listen to Luther, you break into his monologue enough to describe an occasion when Lois demonstrated some real affection for him, her youngest child. Even though he chuckles, tears form and fall. "What am I seeing, boy?" you ask. "Are you crying?" Then the tears really start to flow. Luther shakes his head and begins to describe the purity of his mother's love for him. At this point you find him thoughtful and amenable to most any inquiry you might have.

The key thing to glean from this exercise is that you essentially asked the same question, "Are you still grieving over your mother's death?" in three different ways. Your question for Valerie ("You're still so sad about your mom's passing, aren't you?") is aimed at her *emotions*. Your question for Arthur ("Do you know that you're crying?") is aimed at his thoughts (*intellect*). Your question for Luther ("Are you crying?") is aimed at his actions (*behavior*). You know your family members well (not as well as you're about to). Thus, as you think about how to approach them with questions, you may achieve the best results if you decide whether your most sensitive questions should be emotional, intellectual or behavioral in their nature. This takes some practice, and it probably isn't necessary for the great majority of interactions you'll have with family members. It's a fun process to learn and experiment with, however. It isn't as difficult as it might seem at first and opens lots of doors in lots of conversations. Ultimately, I would predict, this ability to aim your questions emotionally, intellectually or behaviorally will be a great help when you are facing those extremely sensitive, pivotal moments when you're asking the one all-important question you're sure to face.

"Wait," you may protest, "if I ask my folks some of those tough questions about our family, they may get upset. In fact, I know they will get upset. How can I avoid that?"

Actually, you don't want to avoid those emotional explosions—at least, you don't want to avoid causing them. Those outbursts are an indication of the reality that you are succeeding. They are often, in truth the first steps in bringing healing.

During the time I was a hospital chaplain intern, One of my areas of responsibility was the thoracic surgery ICU. I often spoke there with open-heart surgery patients, their families and the medical providers who cared for them.

Way back in the 70s, any heart surgery was regarded as a lot more experimental and risky than the relatively commonplace event it has become in the decades since. The level of stress in the ICU was pretty great; and, as a result, there was often friction between the providers. While most folks who work in that sort of setting will tell you that surgeons are "prima donnas," there was in that ICU one thoracic surgeon who was constantly a total jerk to the nurses who kept his patients alive after he operated on them.

Though I had heard that he possessed this propensity, it took my breath away when I saw it for myself firsthand the morning he spent a good ten minutes berating a nurse. For her part, she did not respond to him. She scurried around the cubicle, administering medicine, observing the patient's vital signs and going through the necessary post-op protocols necessary to care for the doctor's patient. I listened carefully, trying to determine exactly what this nurse had done incorrectly so as to become the butt of this tirade. Eventually I realized she hadn't done anything wrong, that it was just her day to endure the surgeon's wrath.

The chaplains and nurses had access to the same break areas, and later in the day I encountered that nurse while she was purchasing a snack and a soft drink. After greeting her, I asked casually if the surgeon was typically as mean and degrading to her as he had been that morning. Instantly the nurse smacked her soda onto the table and launched into an outraged rant about the doctor Her eyes wide, her face flushed, she raged on for several minutes about the treatment she and other nurses received from that surgeon.

I was terrified, in fact nearly panic-stricken. Having let this "genie out of the bottle," I had no idea what to say to calm the nurse. So I just sat there, horrified at what I had done, listening.

Turns out that was exactly the right response. After venting for three or four minutes, she took a deep breath and smiled. "Wow," she said quietly. "I guess that's been coming on for a while." She took a drink of her soda. "I really don't care for that guy."

There are great lessons here for those of us who start investigating our families. When the questions we ask touch areas that are sensitive and that provoke an emotional response, we should realize we have just heard something of real significance. We should not have the idea that we have done something wrong—although you *will* feel guilty at first. In fact, *the spontaneous release of emotion typically has a freeing, empowering effect on those who express it (*even if it sort of spooks those who witness it*).*

So if we're not supposed to feel guilty or quench the emotional explosions we spark, how are we supposed to react to them? First, we listen. What someone says in that emotional moment may be the most important thing he or she has said to anyone in a long, long time.

Second, we reveal to them we comprehend what they are saying. I think the best way to do this is to remain silent, maintain eye contact and nod or speak quietly when it is appropriate. Another way to do this is via *active listening*. Essentially active listening is paying close attention to a speaker and repeating back what that person has said to you using different words, so they'll know you understand what they've expressed.[xii]

Third, we accept without judgment whatever we are told. Chances are you're going to hear some truly unexpected information involving people you know and are related to (we'll talk about this at length in the next section). One key job of real importance is for us to remain as non-judgmental as possible ("So, Grandma, I hear you saying Uncle Theodore quit coming to family reunions because he's got six felony warrants against him for bank robbery and he's on the run. I didn't know that. That is so interesting.").

Fourth, we take all the time necessary to hear them out. This will likely prove to be an unforgettable, sometimes life-changing moment for them and we need to give them that moment. Your willingness to "give them space" during this process will 1) elevate you as an individual and as a family member in their sight, and 2) will give you "tickets" to speak with them again if you need to come back for more information.

Well, that about covers the topic of using questions to investigate your family as you build your family gram. Oh, there is one other thing I wanted to bring up. . . . And that's how you do it. Such a sly, little introduction is called the **circle-back** or the **Columbo Question**.

If you're not old enough to have seen the old TV series *Columbo*, or if you never paid much attention to it, you can easily find episodes of it via the internet or perhaps a streaming service. Peter Falk played the rumpled police detective Lt. Columbo, who exhibited many distinctive, dependable characteristics as he solved murders. Near the end of his investigations, almost always there would come a moment when he would ask the person he suspected of being the perpetrator a series of fairly innocuous questions, which seemed to satisfy and conclude his work. Then, as he closed his little notebook, he would say, "Well, that about wraps it up. Oh, there is one other thing I wanted to ask you about." Then he would ask a question for which the suspects were never prepared, a question that left them defenseless and started the unraveling of their alibis.

This strategy, disarming one's adversary by distracting and diverting their attention, has been used over the centuries not just by make-believe TV detectives, but by chess grandmasters, courtroom attorneys and military commanders. It was most famously used by Gen. Norman Schwarzkopf during the first Gulf War in 1991 when he used a great buildup of U.S. Marines on the Iraqi seacoast, only to have the U.S. Army mount a land-based attack from the Arabian border (the Marines, by the way, are always itching for a fight and didn't much like being used as a distraction).

By now you're likely saying, "You know, my family history is not a murder investigation or a game or any sort of conflict. Regardless of our past disputes, I don't want to view my family as 'adversaries.' In fact, that's part of what I'm trying to overcome."

A couple of things here: first, if the sort of information you're seeking was easily obtained and obvious, this sort of pursuit wouldn't be necessary. The most valuable treasures are typically buried, and it takes a little work to unearth them. Second, as we'll see going forward, many of the people you'll speak to in your family aren't aware they possess or that they are concealing information you need. Asking for that information in just the right way can release a flood of marvelous detail that otherwise would remain unintentionally concealed.

One of the great examples of this dynamic was Alex Haley's interview with the Black Muslim activist Malcolm X. At their first meeting, Malcolm was quite reserved and Haley had real difficulty in getting substantial answers to his questions. As their allotted interview time was drawing to a close, Haley casually asked Malcolm a question about his mother. Suddenly the iconic black leader grew emotional. He began to talk at length about his mother, whom he admired deeply. The two men consequently developed a trusting relationship, resulting in Alex Haley becoming the ghost writer of *The Autobiography of Malcolm X*, one of the most noteworthy memoirs of the 20th century. In describing that initial interview, Haley said the only emotion he had seen early in the conversation came when he mentioned Malcolm's mother. Haley stored away that bit of awareness and then circled back and asked the question that opened a door resulting in personal and historical significance.

One can only prepare to a certain extent for interviewing family members. Often the most valuable and interesting, enlightening and empowering information shared comes as a result of circling back around to that casual remark or that curious description that your relative glosses over or hurries past. I find it works well to make a mental note—or even scribble it down so you don't forget it—and come back to that topic once the interviewee thinks the session is about over: "That's about it. Oh, there was one other thing I wanted to ask you about."

Cemetery Tours

How clearly I remember standing beside my father one cool

Sunday morning in a little church cemetery in northern Kentucky. We had been moving slowly from one headstone to another, marveling at how many of our relatives were buried in proximity to one another. Dad stopped abruptly when we happened at last upon a particular marker he had been searching for.

"This is my great-great-grandfather," he said. He studied the two shorter stones on either side of the tall one in the center. "I had no idea he had been married, widowed and married again." After a moment, he continued, "I wonder which of his wives was my great-grandmother."

It's one thing to read about an experience like that. It may result in a profound emotional impact, however, to live through it. In my experience, family cemetery tours are almost always equal measures of enlightenment and mystery.

Dad wasn't the only one who had a real surprise awaiting as a result of a family cemetery tour. My mom was in for a jolt as well when the two of us took my grandmother to visit her family plot. As I strolled down the row of markers, I came to a simple, very small one. The birth and death dates revealed that this relative of mine, whose name I had never heard, was only a small child at the time of his death.

"Mom," I called, "who was Leonard?"

She and my grandmother joined me at the grave, and we did a little mathematics and a little deducing. At a certain point, my mother and grandmother faced one another in wonder. Grandma was in her 80s and Mom in her 60s. Neither had realized they had a brother/uncle who had died in his infancy decades before Grandma was born. Yes, cemetery tours are equal parts of enlightenment and mystery.

For these two reasons, the family cemetery tour is a wonderful tool to use in investigating your family. I recommend taking along older members of your family when possible. Standing at the graves of deceased loved ones tends to spark remembrances. As you listen to these memories, new lines of investigation and new questions needing answers will occur to you.

A cemetery tour also tends to legitimize your investigation in the minds of your relatives. Visits to the cemetery can be remarkably freeing in their own right, even before you begin to look systematically at the information you've acquired.

Once you have visited the cemetery and acquired a whole new list of questions, you'll have good reason to go to other family members and involve them in your investigative work as well. This will also engender some curiosity about why you're asking about the family and what surprising things you might have discovered.

Akin to the cemetery tour is the keepsake tour. You may find that discussions of family history and deceased family members often result in your relatives producing that special box that is kept in the top of the closet, in the attic or under the bed. In it you'll find old photos, certificates, newspaper articles and such memorabilia that can greatly advance your investigations. Consider that this is precisely the purpose for which those keepsakes have been retained. As you peruse those precious items, you may discover the casual conversation and bittersweet recollections that accompany the moment to be a rich source of inadvertently shared information. Remember how Josh Wilson during a discussion with his aunt accidentally stumbled onto the realization that he, a Christian minister, actually descended from a Jewish background.

Another Family Gram

Talbot family description: As we look at the family gram below, let's focus on *Carla*, born in 1974, who is just to the left center of the diagram. Note that she is the child of *Donovan* and *Karen*, who are divorced; Donovan left the family home when Carla was in her teens. The generation of Karen's parents is also included, revealing that *Sam*, Carla's grandfather, is deceased (he was a victim of suicide). Karen's grandmother is *Louisa*. While Carla is close to Louisa, she has a very conflicted relationship with her mother, Karen. Carla has two brothers: *Donny*, one year older, is developmentally handicapped and depends on public assistance; *Ray*, two years younger, is a high school dropout who continues to live at home with their mother Karen after his divorce from *Nita*. Carla has been married twice: she had one son, *Dolph, Jr.*, in her brief marriage to his father *Dolph, Sr.* Like his father, Dolph, Jr., has had continual run-ins with the police ever since he became a teenager. In her second marriage, to *Jake*, she has had three children: *Louise*, an outstanding student who received a partial college scholarship and with whom Carla has always been close;

Jacob, a high school dropout who is the father of Carla's grandchild, *Jacob III*, with *Ashleigh*, his former girlfriend; and *Meagan*, a quiet, studious child. In terms of their vocations, Sam was a farm worker and Louisa owned a general store. In the generation of Carla's parents, Donovan was a carpenter and Karen was a bookkeeper. In the next generation, Dolph, Sr., was a day laborer; Carla, a college graduate is an insurance actuary; and Jake works as an auto body painter. What patterns do you notice in this genogram? What might be important about handing down names?

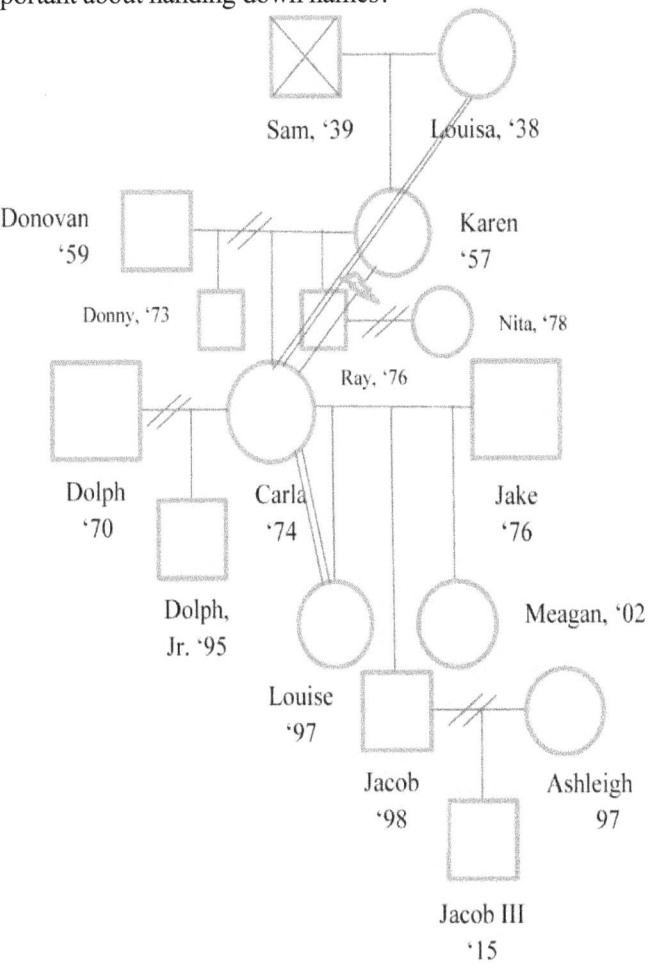

Dr. Mike Simpson

Key Ideas set forth in Chapter Two:
- A key tool to help investigate and understand your family is the creation of a diagram of the various generations, that we call "the family gram."
- To understand your family, it's helpful to use the "emotional distance scale," asking, "How emotionally close are the people in this relationship? Are they fused? Are they estranged? To which of these two extreme are they closer?" The point is not to judge, but to describe them.
- To understand your family, it's helpful to use the conflict scale, asking the question, "How do those in each relationship handle their differences? Are they in "constant chronic conflict," or are they "super reasonable" and avoid conflict altogether? To which extreme are they closer?" Again, the point is not to judge or evaluate relationships, but to describe them.
- Learning to ask "the right questions" in "the right way" will be a tremendous boon to investigating your family. It's important to remember there are at least three ways to ask the same question; a question can be asked in an *emotional* way, an *intellectual* way or a *behavioral* way.
- Often the act of asking questions may lead to emotional outbursts from those you are questioning. In such cases, you have not failed (assuming you weren't trying to get them upset intentionally—which is not nice), rather you have tapped into a vein of long-constrained emotions, which can be healing in itself.
- It's important to develop your ability to ask questions in non-threatening ways, but to pay such close attention to the answers that you will be able to "circle back" to significant issues and investigate them further.
- One of the most revealing and effective tools you can use to investigate your family is the "cemetery tour" of the burial sites of deceased members, making certain to take other family members with you when possible.

3
Who Are These Strange People (I've Known All My Life)?

As the story goes, rock collector Roy Whetstine of Longview, Texas, was visiting in Tucson, Arizona, in February, 1986. He decided to attend a rough gem show, mostly because his two young sons had each sent along $5 in case he found something at the show that he thought might be valuable. As he walked among the various displays, he stopped at the table of one exhibitor, gazing casually at a potato-sized stone sitting in a Tupperware container.

"You want $15 for this one?" Whetstine asked the exhibitor.

"Tell you what," came the reply, "I'll take $10 for it since it's not as pretty as the others."

Whetstine produced the two fives his sons had given him, pocketed the rock and tried to walk out of the show as calmly as possible.

What he had realized, and clearly the exhibitor had not, was that the light blue stone was, in fact, a star sapphire—as it turned out, the world's largest star sapphire. Now adorned with the name the "Life and Pride of America," the 1,905-carat stone was appraised at $2,280,000.

What does this have to do with fixing your family? Just this: to the exhibitor, the rock in the Tupperware box was only distinct from the others he had for sale in that it was not quite as pretty. To the trained eye of Roy Whetstine, it was hugely valuable because he knew what he was seeing. Just so, this chapter of *Fix Your Family* is intended to help you take the information you have been collecting and use it to help you understand your family with the same clear, accurate focus that a true gemologist has for precious stones. As you proceed through this chapter, you may discover that your family becomes "transparent" to you. Their motives and the sources of their motives will become apparent. You will also become much more aware of how you fit into the dynamics of your family relationships. While we haven't gotten around to the actual mechanics of fixing your family yet, many people who begin to understand their families in this way find that their anxiety decreases markedly. Just understanding the real bases for the issues your family faces has a way of engendering peace of mind, like hearing from the doctor exactly what is causing the pain in your side, even before they remove your gall bladder.

One important caution, however: just because you will see your family in a new light and understand them in ways other family members do not, *it is not yet time for you to embark on "fixing your family."* If you rush out and begin to share the insights you have gained with family members ("Guess what, Linda, I just figured out why Aunt Bea has always treated you better than the rest of us!"), you will, in fact, make your work more difficult. I encourage you, before you try to change pernicious patterns of behavior among your kin, to read each of the next two chapters. I promise you that, along the way to planning and creating positive change in your family, you'll very likely learn a lot and have a lot of unexpected fun.

Your Family Saga

"Humanity was created because God loved stories." —An ancient Semitic proverb, reworded.

The first things to watch for as you review the data you've accumulated about your family are **patterns, themes** and **recurring similarities**. Every family is a story and over the course of generations, those stories become a saga. Like all lasting sagas, *the history of your family will have recurring themes*. Recognizing and reflecting on those themes is an essential part of understanding the unique mind sets, understandings and behaviors that have become imprinted within your family.

One excellent example of this is the Ford family. As of this writing, the Executive Chairman of Ford Motors is William Clay "Bill" Ford, who is the great-grandson of Henry Ford, the founder and first president of Ford Motors and the representative of the fourth consecutive generation from his family to sit at the helm of this giant, enduring auto producer. Bill Ford is also the great-grandson of Harvey Firestone, progenitor of Firestone Tire and Rubber Company. As we think about all the family members before him whose lives and careers revolved around automobiles and the family business, it's almost impossible to imagine him doing anything else.

The reality is, however, that virtually every family has repetitive themes. Did you notice the patterns in the Donaldson and Tabor family grams as you looked at their diagrams? We'll discuss each of them below so we can lift up several of the themes and ask what significance they might have for the families. Some of the repetitive themes in families are insignificant and incidental; some, both positive and negative, are profoundly important.

It's also worth noting that there are a lot of different ways for a pattern to be established (in addition to inheriting the family business). One of the silliest and yet most revealing stories about this is what I call the "Pot Roast Inheritance." I've heard this anecdote repeated over the years by a number of folks, but I think I read the original version of it in Dr. Edwin H. Friedman's book *Generation to Generation*:

A mother was teaching her young daughter how to cook various meals and in the process demonstrated how to cook a pot roast. She explained that she took the raw meat and sliced a portion off one end, threw that piece away and cooked the rest. The daughter interrupted her and asked why she cut the end off the pot roast. Mom searched her memory for an explanation and couldn't come up with an answer apart from, "Well, that's the way my mother taught me." The daughter suggested that they call the grandmother and ask why it was necessary to cut the end off the roast before cooking it. Curious now herself, the mother got Grandma on the phone, explained what was happening and asked, "So why am I supposed to cut the end off the roast before cooking it?" Grandma roared with laughter and responded, "I don't know why you cut off the end of *your* roast, but I had such a small pot that I had to cut the roast to get it in."

If the granddaughter had not asked that question, there is no telling—in this age of oversized pots—how many generations of cooks in that family would have begun their supper preparations by hacking off the perfectly good end of a pot roast. The reality is, themes in families can pop up for a multitude of reasons and when they do, they tend to persist, whether those patterns serve a useful purpose or not. Those themes themselves, however, may prove to be extremely useful to you as you grow to understand the uniqueness and vagaries of your family.

Begging your indulgence in advance, allow me to illustrate this with an example from my own heritage. One of the themes within my own family of which I'm especially proud is that, on both sides, I'm a descendant of "pioneer women." Going back as far as it's feasible in the historical record, it's quite clear that the women both on my mother's and my father's side of our family were strong-willed, independent and perseverant. Nancy Jane Croco, my great-great-great-grandmother on the maternal side was a landowner in rural Indiana who sold that property and used it to homestead land in central Kansas. My father's mother, whose father died when she was three, lost her first husband and a child in the great 1918 flu epidemic; she went on to pool her surviving children with my grandfather, who had lost his wife as well, and raised fourteen children to adulthood in the face of extreme hardship.

I'm proud to say that I see these same strong, fearless traits abundantly in succeeding generations as well, for instance in my mom. Mother, at this writing, is a widow in her mid-90s who lives alone on a farm in central Oklahoma. Even at this age, she bears the toughness and contrarian spirit of a true pioneer woman. At family gatherings, we used to joke among ourselves that the way to get any difficult task accomplished perfectly and quickly was to tell my mother that she couldn't do it. In fact, there is only one thing my mother truly fears: speaking aloud to strangers.

Here is my understanding of how that developed: my mother's mother, Cleo, was also a pioneer woman. Rheumatic fever left Grandma profoundly deaf before she was school age. Her parents, bless their hearts, refused to allow her to leave home to attend the Oklahoma School for the Deaf. Cleo grew up reading on about a fourth-grade level. Married at fifteen, she never learned to drive a car, never experienced any meaningful degree of education and never participated in the sort of social activities that most of us take for granted. Despite this, she was incredibly creative, resourceful and optimistic. She raised six healthy, beautiful children to adulthood with the relatively meager resources provided by my grandfather, who was a farmer and a mechanic.

Beginning when my mother was seven or eight-years-old, her

Fix Your Family

older brother would go out to work in the fields with Grandpa, making Mom the oldest child in the house. In those waning days of the Great Depression, there was still an abundant supply of homeless men wandering about the countryside. Periodically some fellow would amble down the farm road and see the well-kept house with flowers growing around it and decide to come to the door and ask for a handout. Mom would see these guys walking toward the house, get Grandma's attention and explain what was happening. Grandma responded, just before shutting herself in a closet, by telling Mom to keep the screen door locked and to tell the stranger that there was no food in the house and no grown-ups around. So, dutifully, my mother—scraggly, skinny little girl—went to the door and dealt with these strange men who were passing through, about whose true nature and designs she had no knowledge whatever.

The first time I heard that story, I was quite upset. The more I thought about it, the more I understood three things. First, it was an act of survival on the part of Grandma. She feared that a pretty, deaf young woman with no man to protect her might prove too much of a temptation for a fellow just passing through. On the other hand, she hoped these strangers wouldn't bother a scrawny, little kid who was home alone. I would say as well, every outrageous action you discover about your family—as hurtful and ill-conceived as it might seem now—was in some way an act of survival. Second, once I heard that this had happened more than once, I understood perfectly why my mother, pioneer woman that she is, remains to this day afraid of speaking in front of strangers. And, third, you remember my saying I was designated early on as the family spokesman? My mom never made me stand up in front of strangers while she hid in a closet; but in the same way she became Grandma's spokesman, I grew up just knowing I was the designated speaker for her and for my family. You ask about my own firstborn son,? Oh, his first job out of law school was as a defense attorney.

The patterns and themes in your family are like pathways that can lead you to a deep understanding of why your family is the way it is. Potentially they can demonstrate where the stuckness is in your family. Eventually, as you will see, these patterns will show you the way to attack and undo that stuckness.

Dr. Mike Simpson

Let's take a moment and reflect on the *Donaldson family gram* from the preceding chapter (p. 26). Did you see any repetition among the members? The first thing you might have noticed is the repetitious use of names: in the earliest generation pictured and in the last generation pictured, the unusual name Astrid appears; in that earliest generation, the middle name of Grandma Anita Rene is handed down to her granddaughter, Rene. That might seem incidental ("You have to give kids a middle name, you know."). But in my experience 1) the kid in a family who ends up with an inherited name is a "loaded child"[xiii] and 2) the parent or grandparent who hangs that family name on the child has a special position within the family and will have a special relationship with the child. For instance, the family gram notes that Sonny is very close to his mother. On the other hand, he has a conflicted relationship with his stepdaughter, Lea. The relative importance of facts like these depends on the family itself. In the case of the Donaldson family, Lea's difficulties with her stepfather caused her to marry and move away from the home at a very early age. You might even wonder if naming her daughter Astrid was Lea's way of affirming her mother's side of the family.

While we're talking about Lea, you might note that—like her mother Trish—Lea is once-divorced. In the case of Trish, Lea was the child of her relationship with Charlie. The toddler Astrid came into the world after Lea's second marriage. As you examine patterns in your family, you may be surprised at how often the makeup of a family constellation repeats itself. You may also find that the history of a family repeats itself down through generations. There are any number of ways that one generation can repeat the actions/behaviors of previous generations. It may be the case, for example, that a family constantly moves from one geographical location to another; we might assume this is not a family pattern, that perhaps the career of the head-of-the-house requires it—except a reflection on the previous generation reveals the same sort of wanderlust. Perhaps every grandchild in a given clan comes from a blended family. Perhaps a grandmother watches a granddaughter working on needlepoint, then goes up to the attic to retrieve and display her own handiwork that the granddaughter knew nothing about until that moment.

It's easy to think that such themes and patterns emerge from genetics or even subconscious suggestions. Maybe to a degree that's true. It's also astonishingly true that themes continue in generations where there was no conscious awareness or even exposure to the preceding generation. One of the best examples of this, and forgive me again for being personal, comes from my own family investigations. I had been an ordained minister for a dozen years before I discovered to my amazement that my great-grandfather, Will Hodam, had also been a preacher. The choice (or calling) of the ministry was nothing I ever discussed with any member of my family prior to surprising everyone when I announced my intention to study for the ministry. I certainly never mentioned it to Grandma. Even though she was a church-goer, I never at any time discussed faith, theology or any professional leaning I might have had with her. Another dozen years passed before I read an extensive family history, in which I discovered that Grandma's great-grandfather, Hugh Sharon Barnhill, had also been a preacher. Yep. Every four generations, my family kicks out a minister. Decades hence some great-grandchild of mine—who likely will never have heard my name—will become a preacher. Themes and patterns are uncanny (that is, unpredictable, unplanned and unconscious), and they occur in every family.

Now let's take a moment to look at the Talbot family gram (p. 42). You'll note it covers parts of five generations. For the sake of clarity in description, we'll use Carla (who's just a little to the left of the center of the diagram) as our focal person; indeed, she is the person who is most interested in investigating and healing her family. What patterns do you notice?

Once again we see names being handed down across the generations; in fact, there are five instances of it among these sixteen individuals. There are also a number of marriages and committed relationships that produce one or more children and then dissolve. If we were looking at other significant dates like marriages, separations and divorces (as you will in your own family genogram), you would see that these couples are universally very young when they get together and, with some exceptions, those first relationships tend not to last.

Another theme you cannot see just from the scant information provided for the Talbots has to do with the relative authority possessed by the women as opposed to the men. For instance,

Dr. Mike Simpson

Louisa, her daughter Karen and granddaughter Carla were all women who "ruled the roost." Each of them in some way was the key financial provider for the household. This tradition seems to be perpetuated in the education and the drive possessed by Carla's two daughters, each of whom seem to be overachievers. By contrast, the men and boys among the Talbots tend to be unmotivated and fairly undependable; the males have universally seemed glad to let the women make the decisions and be the achievers. This was true for Sam, who was generally viewed before his suicide as being henpecked and hapless. It was true of Carla's father, Donovan, who left Karen and moved into a dilapidated apartment, living alone until he found another woman who was willing to take him in and care for him. Carla's first husband, Dolph, ended up running afoul of the law, putting Carla in the position of leaving him, fearing he would be a bad influence on their toddler son, Dolph, Jr. To Carla's dismay, Dolph, Jr. turned out to be a slacker who dropped out of high school in his first year. Jake, Carla's second husband, is a dependable worker, but not interested in furthering his education or career. Jacob, Jake's firstborn son and namesake, managed to fail scholastically as well, dropping out in his senior year, though he did succeed in getting his girlfriend, Ashleigh, pregnant and moving her temporarily into the family's basement before she left him and the baby. Based on the theme we can see prevalent among the men in Carla's family, what sort of behavior would you expect from Jacob's son, Jacob III? Maybe one way to express it is: based on the patterns of several generations, everyone in Carla's family would have much higher expectations for the female children than for the male children. Thus we see, *patterns and themes can also be predictive*; and, again as we've learned, *the past formats the future*.

Based on this notion, below please see a bonus family gram of a make-believe family with three daughters. Let's play "Pick the Favorite." Looking at the little information presented, which of these three daughters would you imagine would be the favorite (and, yes I know, parents aren't supposed to play favorites)?

Fix Your Family

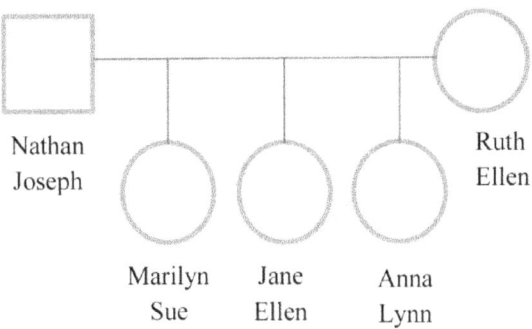

If you selected the child that shares a middle name with her mother, you are right on target. And isn't it interesting that this child was selected at birth to be the favorite? Very likely, this was an "uncanny" process—Mom didn't realize that's what she was doing. This means that *factors beyond a parent's conscious, intentional control can dictate how a child is treated*. Ever hear that saying, "He treated his son like a red-headed stepchild"? Yeah. It might also be the case that Mom's unconscious selection of a particular daughter to be her favorite might cause Dad to single that child out as the least liked. In the fifth chapter, we'll see examples of this undeserved selection and also how to deal with it in a constructive, loving way in the Post/Tucker vignette.

While we're looking at this little diagram, let's note as well that *birth order can be a remarkable predictor of family roles*. This is not news to anyone who has read up on family development, psychology or counseling. It has long been well-established that the order in which you were born can have a determinative impact on how you interact with your family and with the world at large. The first time I was personally aware of this dynamic—and as a firstborn, it made perfect sense to me—was when I read an article pointing out that all but one of the seven Mercury astronauts (the first group of Americans to fly into outer space) were firstborn sons.

Here is a simple, conventional breakdown of how birth order impacts our family roles: firstborn children tend to be more responsible, higher achievers who are empowered to carry on family traditions. Lastborn children tend to have less responsibility (you always knew your kid brother got away with many things you go punished for, didn't you?) and to be empowered to engage in interaction; they seem to group together socially more easily. Middle children tend to be the emotional "shock absorbers" of the family, empowered to accept the anxiety of the family; this tends to result in middle children being the "black sheep," the one who "acts out" in ways the other children don't. Only children—those with no siblings—are viewed as "wild cards," who may take on the characteristics of any or all of the three birth orders.

Ralph had a very traditional nuclear family. Because he had a good job, his wife Betsy was able to be a stay-at-home mom (just like both of their mothers) and raise their three kids, Ralph Jr., Marty and Laura. Every weekday evening when the children were young, Ralph would come home to find a home-cooked supper waiting. As they sat at the table, Ralph would ask Ralph, Jr., what he had done during the day. Almost invariably he would find some little fault with his firstborn's description of his actions, or perhaps he would want to give him some helpful advice so that he could "avoid the problems I had when I was your age." This advice or criticism would often devolve into a lecture and, depending on the degree of Ralph's seriousness (that is, the madder he was), often the middle child, Marty, would act out in such a way as to draw attention to himself. He would start talking loudly; he might belch or pass gas; he might even spill his food or his milk. Abruptly Ralph would stop lecturing Ralph, Jr., and start criticizing Marty's behavior. Eventually he would seem to get tired or finish his rant, then invariably he would turn to the youngest child, Laura, and ask, "Hi, baby. How was your day?"

Betsy was the person who described this dynamic to us. She had come to believe that the ritual described above was detrimental for everyone at the table. As she watched the routine, she felt excluded and helpless. We gave her some suggestions as to how to break up this pattern and to insert/assert herself into the flow of the supper conversation (to everyone's benefit). In the next chapter, we're going to talk about empowering you to emerge as the person who can break up patterns that might not be helpful for your family's growth and happiness.

Speaking of which, remember the generic title we gave to

repetitive, unproductive problems in the family? We said that families get **stuck**, and Betsy's family was definitely stuck. Knowing as you do how much I like acronyms and anagrams, here is a little word play that will help you remember this highly technical term and idea: *Stuck means "Same Tired, Unworkable Concepts and Kinships."*

Before we depart the topic of themes and patterns, we should note that *the use of patterns and behaviors is an important method used by families to maintain* **homeostasis**, or to say it another way that doesn't sound so much like a dread disease, *to achieve and hold onto* **emotional balance**. What is homeostasis/emotional balance?

The simplest way to demonstrate this phenomenon is to ask, when was the last time you heard somebody voice the question, "Are you okay?" Why did they ask and what does that question mean?

Watch children on a playground who are romping and having fun, and it won't take long before one child gets smacked by another child or tumbles off a slide or collides with another child while running. There is a momentary pause, and then the kid realizes that she or he is hurting and begins to cry. Immediately playmates will come to the child and ask, "Are you okay?" Now, the child is conscious, not bleeding and no bones are protruding from the skin; so, in that sense, the other children and any adult watching knows the child doesn't need medical attention. "Are you okay?" really means, "Can you regain emotional balance so we can keep playing, or will you have to have more time to recover?"

This is the same question family members ask one another as they are leaving the funeral home after planning the service of a deceased loved one; the same question other family members ask the bride, mother of the bride, father of the bride, sister of the bride, etc., who bursts into tears ten minutes before a formal wedding ceremony is about to begin; the same question family members ask one another after they leave the ICU cubicle of a loved one or any courtroom proceeding. Whenever we ask, "Are you okay?" or "Are you alright?" or "Are you good?" we are asking someone whether or not they will be able to maintain or regain emotional balance.

Dr. Mike Simpson

Emotional balance can be defined as a relatively unchanging, dependable state of stability that human beings universally require in order to live in the typical manner to which they have become accustomed. We depend upon emotional balance both as individuals and also as families.

There are several important things to observe about emotional balance. First, each person and each family has his/her/its own unique state of emotional balance. I remember having a co-worker who constantly maintained a nearly unachievable list of tasks, to each of which she assigned a challengingly close deadline. When I asked her why she chose to work this way, her response was, "This is how I like it, one notch below panic." Other people "stress out" and become unable to function when they feel overwhelmed. This holds true for families as well. One family is only "comfortable" if they are incredibly busy; another family loses the ability to work together when things become too hectic or when an emotional crisis develops.

Second, it's also the case that a shifting emotional state itself is a form of balance for some individuals and their families. That is the case, for example, with some bi-polar people whose families have become accustomed to a six-week cycle in which everyone endures the mood swings of the "patient."

Dr. Murray Bowen, the psychiatrist who first recognized and investigated all these realities we are studying, stumbled onto the whole concept of emotional process because of this pattern. Bowen was given the task of treating schizophrenic patients. As the patients began to recover, members of their families began to "act out" in emotionally unbalanced ways. He realized that families are emotionally bound and that the schizoid behavior of his patients was actually providing a counter-balance that allowed their families to maintain their emotional equilibrium; accordingly, the families lost their emotional balance when the "crazy" ones quit acting crazy. In this way, the "identified patient" is in reality a sort of pressure valve for the whole family; the more emotional pressure the family experiences, the crazier the patient acts and the rest of the family gets to maintain its balance.

Third, this leads us to the observation that, among other things, families rely on established patterns to maintain the emotional balance of the whole group. Why do certain individuals find they have "unofficially officially" been assigned specific responsibilities within the family, like the young woman we mentioned in Chapter One who had come to hate Thanksgiving, but could not give herself emotional permission to walk away from what she perceived to be her obligation to the family? Why are the same games (actual and emotional) played at every family gathering? Why does everyone in the family adhere to a set of unspoken rules, and new additions to the family are quickly shown the acceptable limits of their behavior? The unspoken, but universal, principle behind this is, "if we all do the same thing we have been doing, then we can mostly ignore the ups and downs, crises and vicissitudes life throws at us and, individually and as a family, we'll all be . . . (wait for it) . . . 'okay.'"

On the other hand, sometimes the themes of the family get violated. If everybody expects Uncle Buford to get drunk and pass out at family birthday parties and Buford, for whatever reason, stays sober, the emotional balance of the family will be challenged. By the way, do the family's expectations make it more difficult for Buford to sober up? If every female member of the clan for five generations has become a teacher and the next in line, Cousin Lucretia, becomes a trapeze artist in a traveling circus, the family will be challenged. The good news about this, as we shall see, is that challenging these themes in a positive way— intentionally upsetting the emotional balance of the family—has the potential to promote healing and unlock new life in your family, heal stuckness and prompt explosions of growth.

Want to Hear a Secret? Promise Not to Tell?

Do you remember I wrote that it dawned on me I had never once heard my father mention my uncle, even though my little sister was named for him? When I began to investigate Dad's family, I discovered only one clear fact was known about the fate of Uncle Leslie: he had disappeared. My father was seventeen at the time and was at home on his parents' farm when the sheriff showed up and said that Leslie's abandoned automobile had been discovered along a county road.

In asking other family members questions about him, I found several other truths—none related to Leslie personally, but rather about how the family dealt with his disappearance. I discovered that, not only had there never been any kind of memorial service for Leslie, in fact there had never been an open family discussion about him after he disappeared; speaking openly about Leslie was taboo. When I freely began to ask family members about him, something no one had done in fifty years, I discovered there had been a fair amount of whispered disinformation; that is, people were actually suggesting things about him that they pretty much knew were not true. And, when I dug down to the real opinions about his disappearance, I discovered there was not just one but actually four different narratives about what might have happened to Uncle Leslie.

If you go back through the two paragraphs above, you may have picked up on three out of the *four varieties of secrets*. What exactly is a secret? *I would define a secret as significant information known to an intentionally limited number of people.* Most of us, when we think about the concept of secrets, think of the simplest form: Stephanie knows something, shares it with Reggie, so Stephanie and Reggie have a bit of information that is not common knowledge. That's your **basic secret**. The second kind of secret is the dissemination of **false information intended to conceal the truth**. For example, when you have to have the vet put down your dog, you probably tell your small children, "Rusty went to live on a farm." The third sort of secret is the **taboo subject**, the situation in which the whole family has certain information (or assumptions), but there is an implicit agreement not to discuss it; everybody knows that Aunt Ethel spent some time in the penitentiary for tax evasion, and everybody knows not to mention it. Fourth is the "secret we keep from ourselves": **denial**.[xiv] Human beings have an astonishing ability to deny truths that are obvious to others around us. Not only as individuals but also as entire families, we can avoid the awareness of inconvenient realities to an amazing degree.[xv]

That there are various types of secrets is significant for us as we investigate our families because much of whatever may be keeping your family stuck is in some way concealed. And based upon the different sort of secrets there are, chances are members of your family don't even realize they are keeping secrets. Certain folks in your family may have hugely important information and honestly don't believe they have anything of importance to share. This is, in fact, an extremely common phenomenon, as we read above in the account of how Josh Wilson, a Christian minister, discovered he was a direct descendant from a conservative Jewish background. His Aunt Velma had no idea she had been passively concealing something that might have a huge impact on others in her family.

So, recognizing how significant these untold truths can be, a question arises as to how hard we should push to unearth them. I think the answer is: *don't be overly aggressive as you try to discover hidden information about your family*. I say this for several reasons. The very act of asking questions about your family's history, first, begins a process of reflection within those kinfolks with whom you'll be speaking. It's often the case they will want to come back to you of their own accord in the future to discuss matters that have newly come to mind. Second, family members who share any information at all with you have become, whether they realize it or not, your allies in investigating your family and by extension in helping to get the family unstuck. If completely followed through, third, this unsticking process very often unleashes a great flood of memories and additionally shared information, so you might end up getting a lot more data about your family than you ever expected. In my view, it's a good thing to ask family members for the information you want and then gratefully accept whatever they supply.

As we alluded above, secrets are not just significant. *Secrets can be explosively powerful*, even life-changing. Ever watch an award ceremony like, for instance, the Motion Picture Academy Awards? I think it's most interesting to watch the faces of those who have been nominated in the moments before the winner is announced. Try as they might to appear casual and uninterested, the attention of the nominees is riveted to the folks holding the envelope because they have information that will irrevocably change their lives.

"Wait a minute," you might say, "most people don't know that others in their families are holding onto secrets. Maybe Cousin Darnell is actually not the child of Aunt Meredith and Uncle Bruce. Maybe Darnell is adopted and even the other children don't realize he's not their natural brother at all. If Darnell and his siblings don't ever find out about it, it's really not all that powerful, is it?"

Dr. Mike Simpson

Ah, yes, it is—not because the secret is told, but more so because it's always possible the secret could be discovered; those keeping the secret know this and thus are living with the stress of potential emotional explosion. Sure, Darnell might go through his entire life thinking Meredith is his birth mother, but the untold secret would very likely have a profound impact in the lives of his stepparents Meredith and Bruce, as well as all those other family members who probably also know this secret. Viewed in this way, we can see that *secrets are potentially explosive*, and you can imagine—if truth be told, you probably know—what it's like to go through your life holding onto something that might blow up at any moment.

Seen in this light, you can recognize that *an important secret is really a sort of "anxiety account."* That is, having an important secret is like opening a little savings account where stress/worry/concern is banked. Every time the thought of that secret comes to mind or the secret is almost revealed or the topic is discussed, a little anxiety is added to the savings account. The more significant the secret, the longer it is kept, the more anxiety it accrues. Periodically one of these anxiety accounts gets cashed in; that is, sometimes a secret is revealed to those who didn't know it. When that happens, people get upset, to be sure, but also there is a spontaneous release of anxiety. It can also be the case that enlightenment and a feeling of relief and freedom sometimes follow the revelation of an important secret. As my teacher Ed Friedman used to say, people don't die from being upset; however, hanging onto an anxiety-provoking secret eventually just might kill you.

An example from Ed's life serves to illustrate this point quite well. He was raised by his mother to believe that his father was nearly a perfect person. Whenever Ed would demonstrate his humanity by making a mistake or falling short of expectations in some way, his mother would remind him that his father never did such things. After he was a grown man, however, Ed discovered that his father, who was the son of a tailor, once got into his father's workshop along with a cousin and the two boys totally destroyed a wedding suit that Ed's grandfather had sewn for a groom—and this happened on the very day the groom was to be married. Stunned, Ed asked his mother why she had concealed this story from him. She replied, quite emotionally, that she didn't want him to grow up to be a naughty boy like his father. After that event, Ed wrote, he had a tremendous feeling of release and empowerment.

Perhaps some secrets held for long periods of time by some folks achieve a kind of break-over point at which their potential for pure emotional explosion is diminished. Still these significant secrets have a hugely transformative power. I would say they are like emotional pearls: in the same way an oyster coats a grain of sand again and again until it becomes a precious jewel, so a long-held secret eventually obtains a priceless luster and an unfathomable power to transform.

Marsha Lynch was eager to sit with her Great-Uncle Horace at the annual summer reunion. Horace was the unofficial family historian, and Marsha was investigating her family. She brought along her spiral notebook with a page devoted to each family unit in the clan and reviewed what she knew about each. Horace had a tremendous memory for dates and relationships and incidental information about family members long deceased.

About the time they finished reviewing the various nuclear families, her great-uncle grew quiet. Softly he asked, "You know, Marsha, we're only half the family."

"What? Half the family?"

He nodded. "Grandpa Calvin had another family."

"What?"

"Yes. He took up with a black woman a few miles over from our family farm. Together they had three or four kids, I'm not sure. He provided for them just like he did for Grandma and his white children."

Astonished, Marsha felt her jaw drop open. "Well, who are they? Are we in contact with them?"

Horace shrugged. "I don't know. I don't think any of us kept up with them after Grandpa died."

Marsha stared at her great-uncle in silence. Whatever she might have expected to learn about her extended family was dwarfed by this astounding revelation. She had no idea what to make of what she had just learned, whether or not she should try to locate Calvin Lynch's second family or how this would impact her investigation.

Oh, yes. Maybe I should have mentioned this: whenever you

start to investigate your family and you begin to help it get unstuck, not only will your family be changed in startling ways, but you are going to be changed as well. You cannot guide your kinfolks on this awakening, empowering journey without taking the trip yourself.

Now That We Have This Secret, What Are We Going to Do With It?

There is an inevitable result of the reality that we all keep secrets and sometimes must share them. Thus results in **a conspiracy**. For our purposes, *let's describe a conspiracy as two or more individuals sharing, planning and possibly acting upon concealed information.* And right away let's make note that a conspiracy is not necessarily a bad thing; we're just describing a basic reality of human interaction. For instance, when Robby and Roberta plan a surprise birthday party for their dad, Robert, that's a benevolent conspiracy. Perhaps you had not realized that, beyond planning surprise parties for loved ones, you are actually part of a great number of conspiracies at any given time. To get a handle on this, we should consider that, just as there are different kinds of secrets, there are different kinds of conspiracies. We can see this in the following vignette.

Randy and Kurt, two young men in their late teens, shared a deep sense of scorn toward Dexter, a slightly-younger teen who attended their high school and very much wanted to be included among their tight circle of friends. Because they thought it would be funny and because they wanted to dissuade Dexter from pursuing them and because they wanted to punish him for being so "beneath" them, Randy and Kurt decided to play a trick on Dexter. They told him in a fraternal tone that Mandy, one of the prettiest and most popular young women in their class, had confided to them that she was very attracted to Dexter and was hoping Dexter would ask her to attend the upcoming homecoming dance.

"You should ask her tomorrow morning before class," Kurt said, "you know, before some other guy beats you to it."

"Make sure you bring her an espresso," Randy said. "She loves Espresso, and that way she'll know how much you care."

Dexter had never believed he had a chance of dating anyone as high up the social ladder as Mandy. Still, as much to please the guys as to win a date with the most beautiful girl he knew, Dexter dutifully showed up before class with an espresso the next morning and approached Mandy, who was holding court with a number of not-quite-so-pretty-as-her girlfriends. He held out the cup to her and mumbled his request to take her to homecoming. Mandy recoiled, horrified at the prospect that her friends might think she would actually associate with someone like Dexter.

"As if!" she exclaimed. "Keep your stupid coffee, you lame loser," she said, just as she turned and walked away.

Her gaggle of attendants marched behind her, turning back to look at Dexter with disbelieving smiles as they giggled and whispered to one another. It had been the intention of Randy and Kurt to keep up the charade by feigning surprise at Mandy's reaction, but the joke had worked so well they couldn't maintain serious expressions.

Roaring with laughter, Randy said, "Seriously, Dex? You asked Mandy? What were you thinking?"

"Yeah, dude," Kurt joined in, "you just got majorly punked."

It took several minutes for the magnitude of his humiliation to take root in Dexter's awareness. When it did, he simply left school, not bothering to go to the office or to speak to anyone about what had happened. The next day and the day after, he stayed in bed, refusing to go to school and also refusing to explain to his very concerned parents what had gotten him so upset.

Kurt had not anticipated the extent of Dexter's negative response to the trick. As the days passed and their victim did not return to school, Kurt began to feel a great deal of remorse—though he knew he could not express his regret in front of Randy or any of their buddies. After lunch one day, he stopped by the school counselor's office to see Miss Lawrence.

"I need to talk to you about something," he said, "but it has to be just between us."

"Does it involve breaking the law or endangering yourself or someone else?" the counselor asked.

"No ma'am."

"Okay then."

Kurt rapidly recounted the entire sordid affair, finishing with a shake of the head and saying, "You know, this wasn't my idea;

but still, Ms. Lawrence, I can't believe Dex took it so hard. Now I feel bad."

Miss Lawrence sat staring at the student. At least she understood why Dexter's parents had called her, quizzing her as to whether or not their son had been bullied. She realized as well, because of Kurt's request, that she had to keep this information in confidence. Indeed, because he had approached her with this story and a request for counseling, her first responsibility was to counsel Kurt. She knew she could not ethically confront Randy about his part of the joke or explain to Mandy how they had also tricked her.

I apologize for taking you back to the dark side of high school. This little tale, however, does a good job of depicting several different forms of conspiracy.

For starters, there is the basic **conscious, intentional conspiracy**: Randy and Kurt conspired together to dupe their wannabe friend Dexter into humiliating himself. This is what we think of when we reflect on the notion of conspiracies. Such conspiracies can be malicious—as everyone involved in this prank discovered—or they can be beautiful. Recently the wife of an old friend of mine suggested the two of them go to supper alone at his favorite restaurant to celebrate his 80th birthday. He arrived to discover that his four children and their spouses were waiting (without any of his grandkids) and that each couple had created a nostalgic, sentimental keepsake gift.

That sort of graceful conspiracy stands in stark contrast to the wicked practical joke Randy and Kurt played on Dexter. Malicious conspiracies almost always result in broken trust and an unwillingness to form trusting relationships. In other words, the trick played by the teenagers permanently impaired Dexter's ability to trust them. Often we hear spouses or others in committed relationships where an affair has occurred (which, after all, is a conscious, intentional conspiracy) talk about the difficulty of rebuilding trust. Benevolent conspiracies, like the birthday gathering described in the previous paragraph, enhance trust, just as all sincere expressions of affection enhance trust.[xvi]

Going back to our vignette, when Kurt approached Miss Lawrence and sought to share with her the story of what he and his friend had done, he drew the counselor into a **conscious,**

unintentional conspiracy. This sort of arrangement is when a person finds herself or himself compelled to keep a secret that originated elsewhere. Obviously, this happens to clergy, counselors, lawyers, health-care providers and other professionals in confidential settings all the time. Apart from a very narrow list of exceptions as referenced by Miss Lawrence above (like violations of the law or the threat of physical harm), when a professional caregiver is told something in confidence, that person is ethically bound to keep the secret, whether he/she wants to or not. And lots of times caregivers don't want to be in that conspiracy. I recall my dismay at learning that a congregant of mine was faking a debilitating physical condition. The entire church membership believed she was handicapped and treated her with deference. I detested the fact that she had placed me in a conspiracy with her from which I could not ethically escape.

Of course, it's not just professional people who find themselves stuck in such conspiracies, is it? Parents, grandparents and other relatives experience this all the time: "Grandma, you got to help me. I got a ticket I can't afford to pay; and if Dad finds out, he'll take my car away." Got the picture? When was the last time you chose to help one family member keep a secret or quietly follow through on a plan so as to keep peace in the family? Conspiracies always involve secrets. Secrets always elevate anxiety. Secrets and conspiracies always create emotional distance between conspirators and those they are conspiring against, making intimacy more difficult and inviting even more secrets/conspiracies.

Conspiracies create strange bedfellows. Several times as a pastor I had the experience of being close friends with one member of a family, only to have a different member of the same family involve me in an unintentional conspiracy against my friend. For instance, let's assume that I had a friend named Tony with whom I played tennis on a weekly basis. And let's say Ginny, Tony's wife, came to me as her pastor and told me in confidence that she had cashed out a savings account the two of them were building and she had used the money to pay off gambling debts. Suddenly I was in the position of conspiring against my friend with his wife. And if he discovered what she had done and wanted to talk with me about it, I would have to feign ignorance of her actions. Unintentional conspiracies have the power to bind us in relationships in uncomfortable ways. They have the potential to destroy the trust we've attained in relationships that are actually much more important to us. It's also the case that sometimes a person intentionally seeks to lock you into such a conspiracy in order to come between you and someone you are close to. In the next chapter, we'll be discussing how to extricate oneself from such pernicious traps.

As powerful and common as these types of conspiracies are, I have to admit in my view they are not the most intriguing forms. Remember Mandy, the beautiful social butterfly Dexter wanted to invite to homecoming? Remember her friends? When Mandy rejected Dexter, those young ladies knew exactly how they were supposed to respond, didn't they? Nobody took them aside and said, "Now when Dexter makes a fool of himself and Mandy humiliates him, you all snicker and mock him, okay?" These girls were complicit in an "unconscious" conspiracy or, as I like to phrase it, an **uncanny conspiracy**: *one that people enter into without intention and often without real awareness.*

Uncanny conspiracies can be benevolent in their intentions.[xvii] For instance, most grownups around the world who participate in the observance of the Christmas holiday are part of an uncanny conspiracy revolving around the existence of a particular, heavy-set fellow from the North Pole. We entered this conspiracy in our elementary school years at about the point we discovered our elders had been engaged in a virtually universal conspiracy concerning this fellow. We went from being objects of the joke, to being in on the joke, to helping to perpetuate the joke. As enlightened children, most of us wouldn't think of revealing the joke to younger children who weren't in on it—in fact, we had hostile feelings toward those who did share the secret with children who had not figured it out on their own. We understand that we are to perpetuate this conspiracy until those who aren't part of it at last grasp for themselves they have been conspired against.

Uncanny conspiracies are amazing to me in that they are extremely common and that, unlike that bit about Santa Claus, many times the folks who are co-conspirators don't even know it. With many uncanny conspiracies, there is a tremendous amount of denial. For instance—and, all things considered, this is a fairly innocuous example—back in the day when I was a church revitalization consultant, I learned that many declining churches are stuck in an uncanny conspiracy. If you were to take the members of a dying church and hook them up to a lie detector and ask them, "Do you want your church to thrive and grow?" the invariable, immediate answer of almost 100% of the members would be, "Yes!" Then those same members would go out and in an uncanny fashion do everything within their power to prevent their churches from attaining new growth and vitality. On some level these church folks shared the awareness that new growth requires change; what they truly wanted was the restoration of their congregations to be exactly as they had been during the golden age of their churches. *Our rational priorities are often not at all our emotional priorities,* and when it comes to groups of people—like families—emotions will invariably win out over rationality (unless the right leader can step forward).

If we extend this idea to your family, we could say it's very likely your family has some unspoken priorities of which they may not even be aware. These priorities are much more emotional than intellectual and thus extremely powerful. Identifying these priorities is a necessity for those who want to fix their families.

A real example of this that hits close to home for me is the emotional dynamic I've mentioned several times already regarding the disappearance of my father's older brother Leslie. There was very much a "conspiracy of silence" regarding his fate. No one went to his parents and dozen siblings and said, "Okay, we aren't going to talk about this." Still everyone in the family knew it was just something you didn't discuss. As a result, Leslie's disappearance was a long-term, unhealed emotional wound. Chances are there may be such taboo subjects in your family. Recognizing what those silent conspiracies are, the history behind them and the people involved is the first step in dealing with them.

Why Aren't There Any Two-Legged Stools?

Here is a great experiment for you that is extremely easy and fun: go to a person you live with or call up someone you know very well and say, "Okay, we're going to have a conversation for five minutes, and neither of us is going to mention another person.

We can only talk about you or me." Assuming you are not on your honeymoon, I predict you cannot easily accomplish this. But let's say you actually do pull it off. Let's up the degree of difficulty: "Okay, we're going to have a two-minute conversation just about us; not about work; not about hobbies; not about movies or music, books or anything on the internet." You probably can't accomplish that either.

The phenomenon here is called **triangling**, which we could define as *two or more people in a relationship achieving emotional balance by focusing on someone or something outside their relationship.* Triangling, in and of itself, is neither a good or bad thing, rather it is simply a reality of the way people must relate to one another. In the same way you cannot sit down on a stool with two legs without falling over, so you cannot maintain a relationship without having something outside that relationship to focus on.

A lot of great insight about triangles and triangling came from Eric Berne, a progenitor of Transactional Analysis, who wrote the well-known book *Games People Play*. Berne discussed what he called the "Persecutor/Rescuer Triangle" or the "Alcoholic Triangle" that he recognized was at work in families of alcoholics. In this situation, the inescapable presence of alcohol dominates the relationship between husband and wife with the non-alcoholic spouse shifting from rescuing the alcoholic to persecuting the alcoholic in a repetitive ritual. Alcohol becomes a sort of "third person" in the relationship, offering a kind of teeter-totter stability—until the progression of the disease destroys the household and life of the addict.

I mention this with the caveat that the alcoholic triangle is an extreme example of a triangle that helps to demonstrate how triangles work. Triangles 1) stabilize a relationship, 2) provide a focus upon something or someone other than the people involved and 3) can shift dramatically and quickly. These characteristics are also true of the healthiest triangles, and we are all continually involved in triangles and triangling. Because triangles are an inevitable aspect of human relationships, it pays to have some understanding of them. In the next chapter, we'll focus on how you can make helpful, healthy changes within the triangles of which you are part.

One of the most counter-intuitive truths (which is to say, it seems just the opposite of what you'd think to be true) about triangles is, *when people in a relationship decide to triangle someone out, it's because the two who are doing the triangling are uncomfortable with their own relationship.* To say that in a somewhat more comprehensible way, when Kurt and Randy decided to "triangle out" Dexter, it was a sign that they were uncomfortable to a degree in their relationship to each other. Likewise, when Mandy's cadre of girlfriends joined in mocking Dexter after his moment of humiliation, it was a sign they were insecure in their relationship with Mandy. We'll call this *the principle of triangular discomfort*. Cool name, huh?

Here is another thought experiment for you: who in your family has triangled out someone else in your family? According to the principle of triangular discomfort, if your cousin Hobart and his wife Heather decided they can no longer stand to associate with his mother, your Aunt Inez, it means that Hobart and Heather have some discomfort with one another.

It's important to note that triangling in and out does not have to be as dramatic, complete and ultimate as the examples we've been using. Often times family members (or co-workers, team members, social acquaintances) unconsciously choose some people from within the group to which they are close and others from whom they will remain distant. That just happens. Also, the degree of intentionality in triangling someone out is an indication of the degree of discomfort within the relationship of those doing the triangling. For instance, if Aunt Lucy and Aunt Bernice go out of their way to exclude their sister, Aunt Cora, from a trip to see their mother—full knowing that Cora will find out about it and feel hurt and hostile—it's not just that Lucy and Bernice are uncomfortable with Cora, but they are also uncomfortable with each other. On the other hand, if Uncle Bud and Uncle Phil don't call their brother, Uncle Walt, to help them build a deck for Bud, it may not indicate anything but that Walt is inept with power tools and they don't want to take him to the emergency room again. So, the more animosity involved in triangling someone out, the more the folks doing the triangling have an unspoken problem with each other.

Triangles and triangling, like so many of the other topics

we've engaged in this chapter, are subjects well-deserving of further study and investigation. For our purposes at this point, the key thing is that you begin to recognize the triangles of which you are a part, recognize the triangles that exist and have existed in your family and understand the dynamics of how those triangles have pulled people closer together and forced people further apart. Soon we'll be suggesting some tools that will empower you to move about within the triangles you're a part of as you wish and to use their existence to help fix your family.

Your Family: Real Star Power

The last topic we need to reflect on in this chapter is your **family constellation**. This is to say, *family members are like planets within a solar system: constantly in movement around one another, moving toward and away from one another and in doing so changing the dynamics of the family itself.*

What I'm describing here is the **physics of human relationships**. In the same way that the earth never stands still, so none of our relationships ever actually stands still. I guess this is why we are always seeking emotional balance; everything keeps moving. *If you consider the most important people in your life, the reality is you are either moving toward them or away from them.* Think about your immediate family. Who is moving toward whom? Who is trying to escape the orbit of whom? If we go back to the notion that those who triangle others out are in fact uncomfortable in their own relationship, this makes perfect sense: if I can focus on animosity I feel toward person C, then I don't have to focus on the fact that I have a hard time trusting and communicating warmly with person B.

There is one particularly important principle I'd like to lift up here: in the family constellation, when person A moves away from person B (that is, person A increases the emotional distance between the two of them), person B will intuitively move toward person A. And, if person A moves toward person B, person B will intuitively move away from person A. This is a matter of emotional balance of the two people involved in the relationship trying to maintain a constant emotional distance from one another.

Based on this we can see that, unlike the actual solar system, *we can choose to move in the direction of others or away from*

Fix Your Family

them. As we will see, it's actually possible to free up all the planets in your solar system so they can renew their positions in the family constellation. In this sense, fixing your family—getting them unstuck—implies giving them the freedom to rework all their relationships, resulting in growth, new insights, new possibilities and lots of joy.

This leads us to the notion of pursuit. *We can say, if someone is moving toward you, they are pursuing you. If you are moving toward someone, you are pursuing them.* When one person is actively trying to move toward another person, the person being pursued has the option of moving toward the pursuer or moving away. Whatever choice the person being pursued makes has an impact on every other person in the family constellation. The most obvious example of this is when Grandpa Joe and Uncle Scott both show up at Thanksgiving. The father and son just don't get along. Joe would like Scott to be closer, but also doesn't want to bless any of the living choices Scott has made. Scott would like to be closer, but he doesn't want to let his father dictate how he lives. Meanwhile everyone in the family is holding her or his breath while waiting to see how the turkey is going to get carved, so to speak.

A big part of being successful in fixing your family has to do with "inviting people to pursue you." When people are pursuing you, they are much more open to your insights, your suggested actions and requests. There is a real art to inviting folks to pursue you, and our intention is to turn you into someone your family finds emotionally irresistible—something that ultimately will be a great benefit to all of them.

And now that you've investigated your family and are beginning to grasp the meaning of all the things you've learned, it's time for us to turn our attention to you!

Key Ideas set forth in Chapter Three: these ideas are intended to assist you in understanding the events and relationships you've studied as you've investigated your family.
- Every family is a story and over the course of generations, those stories become a saga. Like all lasting sagas, the history of your family will have recurring *themes, patterns*

and *similarities*.
- Themes and patterns are one method families use to maintain *homeostasis* or *emotional balance*. Emotional balance can be defined as a relatively unchanging, dependable state of stability that human beings universally require in order to live in the manner to which they have become accustomed and feel comfortable.
- One natural process employed by all families to maintain emotional balance is the keeping of secrets. Secrets express themselves as *simple basic secrets, false information intended to conceal a truth, taboo subjects* and *denial*.
- An inevitable outgrowth of secrecy is the development of conspiracies. *Conspiracies* can be conscious and intentional, conscious but unintentional or uncanny—meaning unconscious.
- Another universal emotional process used to maintain emotional balance is *triangling*, which is two or more people in a relationship achieving emotional balance by focusing on someone or something outside their relationship.
- Families are like planets within a solar system: constantly in movement around one another, moving toward and away from one another and in doing so changing the dynamics of the family itself. Just as heavenly bodies respond to the laws of physics, so there are emotional principles we could call the "*physics of human relationships*" that predictively describe how individuals move toward and away from one another in a family.

4
The Person in the Mirror Is the One You're Looking For

Way back in 2004, mostly because I had a commercial driver's license, I was asked to sponsor a group of church kids on a beach trip. On Friday, the last day of our excursion, we let the young people go to the ocean for one last early morning splash, then brought them back to the hotel to get ready for the four-hour drive home. They were all dragging with fatigue from a week at the beach and the exhaustion and exhilaration of a couple of hours in the water. We adult sponsors wanted to get on the road as soon as possible, but none of us had the heart to push these tired kids to hurry.

"Hey," I whispered to the other sponsors, "I've got an idea. Let's tell Marcy we have to be out of here by 10."

Marcy was one of the older members of the youth group. She had no official title or designated role among the kids, but she was the one we could always turn to if we needed results from the youth group. When she came down the hallway of the lodge in her flip-flops, wearing her beach wrap over her bathing suit, we stopped her.

"I don't know what we're going to do, Marcy," one of us said. "Check out time is at 10. That's only twenty minutes. If we don't get the kids out of their rooms and onto the bus, the lodge will charge us for another day."

For an instant she stood staring at us sternly, hands on her hips. Then she began to go to each room occupied by our youth and bark orders. Twenty minutes later, the whole youth group—spic and span and fully packed—was on the bus.

We praised Marcy and bragged about her to her parents and others in the congregation—not that she did it for our appreciation. That's just how Marcy was. In moments when things needed to get done, Marcy was the person to whom you turned. Sometimes I wonder if she ever found out that checkout time wasn't until 11?

Dr. Mike Simpson

Now let's talk about you. Are you like Marcy? Are you able to compel the people around you to do the things you ask? Do you have what it takes to bring about real change? Isn't that why you're reading this book, because you want your family to function better? Of course, it doesn't matter how much usable wisdom and practical advice any book contains if there isn't someone to take these ideas and put them into action in your family. Who's that going to be? It either has to be someone you choose (and to whom you give a copy of *Fix Your Family*) or more likely, it's got to be you. Yes, the person you see in the mirror every morning.

Perhaps, when you think about all the new ideas—many counter-intuitive—forced upon you by this book and add to them all the information and new understandings you've acquired about your family, you might decide you absolutely do not want to be the one to initiate the process of helping your loved ones get unstuck. There is a term for that feeling of "No way! Not me!" It's called "repudiation of calling." And, regardless of whether you are a person of faith or not, you might be interested in knowing that the great majority of biblical figures who accomplished truly significant things—from Moses to Gideon to Simon Peter—all had at least one moment in which they resisted the call to do what needed to be done. So you're in excellent company.

I do not want to understate the emotional impact of following through with planning and executing the unsticking of your family. There will likely be some frustration, confusion, pushback and a couple of anxious moments when your heart will be in your throat. In retrospect, however, the ultimate result of your work will most likely make any dread you might be experiencing pale to insignificance.

Additionally, there are great benefits to learning all about Emotional Process regardless of whether you embark on fixing your family or not, starting with a great diminishing of your own anxiety. Back when I worked primarily with church leaders, it was remarkable to witness the difference between those attending their first Family Systems workshop and those attending their second. Those who came back to attend their second event were amazingly calm. They exuded confidence and curiosity and frequently expressed a feeling that they were more in control of their congregations and their own lives than they had ever been. The same dynamic is available for those who are willing to continue learning the concepts we're sharing and to take the risk of putting them into action in their families.

The remainder of this chapter is intended to discuss the important personal qualities that you'll find helpful as you prepare to help your family get unstuck. Maybe this would be a good time to repeat one of Ed Friedman's famous dictums: "This theory is only true 70% of the time." That was actually, in part, Ed's way of saying that we can't be perfect in achieving the qualities described below. Neither can we always elicit the result we want from our family members, regardless of how well we embody the principles of change. You'll find as you strive to grasp and incorporate these ideas and behaviors that utilizing them becomes a sort of second nature; indeed, you will experience a true "paradigm shift" in the way you relate to your family and they will experience you in a totally different way as well. And if only 70% of the changes you're seeking come about, your family will come unstuck in dramatic ways.

As I reviewed this book again almost ten years after I began writing it, I recognized clearly that this is the daunting chapter. The issue, as I recognize it, is that I'm setting forward not one new skill or quality for you to adopt so you can fix your family. Instead, I've listed nine new abilities for you to grasp, practice and perhaps master. From the outset, this sounds a little like climbing not one peak but a whole range of mountains. Allow me to share a few insights that will help defuse your anxiety about acquiring these qualities.

First, many of these skills hold hands. As you allow yourself to *let go of your anxiety*, you'll find it easier to *have a humorous outlook* on your relationships, which in turn will make it easier to *remain connected*. Second, don't expect to master or even fully grasp all of these principles right away. It's a trial-and-error learning process and no one is grading or judging you. These abilities will begin to emerge in your repertoire as you need them. Ed Friedman advised above all that a leader should be a "non-anxious presence." I wrestled anxiously for several years with how to become a non-anxious leader; don't know if I ever figured it out, but one day my anxiety dissipated and I quit worrying about it. Third, some of these insights and how they relate to your personal experience may burst into your consciousness like a true revelation. I've described my experience the first night I started reading *Generation to Generation*. I did not want to put the book down because I recognized that Family Systems not only could explain why my congregation (and my various unruly families) acted as they did, but how I could work within them to facilitate meaningful change. Fourth, as you attain the ability to understand the actions of those around you from an Emotional Process viewpoint, they will become transparent to you. You will grasp people's true motives (even when they themselves don't). You will be able to predict the responses of others. You will have clarity about why people do the things they do in ways most others do not. It's fun to understand the people around you at a greater depth than everyone else around you. Fifth, Emotional Process/Family Systems is a true paradigm shift. From the outset, it has been not an invention (like a new kind of therapy) but rather a discovery (this is how and why people act as they do). Murray Bowen discovered these principles because of how they worked to treat schizophrenic families. Ed Friedman "mapped" these principles into useful tools for leaders of all types. Mike Simpson mapped them into congregational revitalization. Others have utilized these ideas in a plethora of ways that Bowen never imagined. Thus I say that learning and using the skills, insights and qualities described in this chapter might create new dynamics within you that no one else has imagined. So, please stay with the process.

Getting in Touch with Your Edges

I recall seeing a video of an adolescent group counseling session. The young people were sitting in a circle of folding chairs discussing grief. One of the boys had recently lost his grandfather, to whom he was quite close, and had never dealt with the profound sense of loss that had descended upon him. The counselor was able to encourage him to open up and describe the series of events around his grandfather's death. Then it was suggested that the young man say aloud what he wished he had said to his grandfather before his death. The scene was quite moving.

Sitting next to the boy was a girl who put her hand on him as he began to speak, rubbing and patting his shoulders. The more intense his monologue became, the firmer and more animated the rubbing and patting became. At a certain point, when the boy was "speaking to his grandfather," the counselor got up, went to the girl and took her hand so she could not rub the boy's shoulder any longer.

The counselor recognized that what had started as consolation had in fact become distraction, even to the extent that it would disrupt this cathartic moment of healing for the boy who was speaking. The reason for this was because the girl was totally, inseparably immersed in the boy's grief. Back in the day we used to call this being "co-dependent." For our purposes, we can simply say the girl was poorly defined, or she didn't know where "she ended and the boy began." *The ability to separate yourself emotionally from other human beings around you—to be* **well-defined**—*is the first essential quality you'll need to develop as you move toward fixing your family.*[xviii] In Bowen Theory, being well-defined is typically referred to as "differentiated."

If you consider that the events that cause families to get stuck are emotionally powerful experiences, then discussing and working through those events is going to reveal and release some extraordinarily strong emotions. Going forward, we'll be discussing how to plan intentional events that confront the stuckness in your family; this implies that you'll experience some emotional pushback from the people you care most about. It's also likely that you'll encounter some resistance to the new, different leadership you're about to embody within your family. All of this implies you'll need to be able to stand apart from those around you emotionally. You'll find it important to be able to 1) listen to and interact with family members who are extremely emotional without getting emotional yourself; 2) follow through with the ideas you're proposing and the plans you've set into motion without being dissuaded by angry or timid family members; and 3) anticipate that what you are going to do will be challenged by those who feel threatened, angry and astonished by your behaving in totally unexpected ways.

In a nutshell, you're going to be perceived as a totally different person within your family. To succeed at this, you have to know where you end and others begin. You need to know what problems are yours and what problems belong to others in the family. You need to be aware of how family members have used your emotions against you in the past. You need to resolve that you will not be fodder for the emotional manipulation of others, that any sympathy or even guilt you might feel will not deter you from continuing the work of fixing your family. Let's examine the story of someone who needed to redefine himself and stand his ground emotionally.

Terrance Newell wanted his grandmother to come for a visit. Mrs. Darla Watkins, Terrance's maternal grandmother, had never traveled more than 150 miles in any direction at any time during her 85 years. She had never been on an airplane, never been on a train, never been outside the state of Kansas and never visited the homes of any of her grandchildren who had moved away from Wichita.

Growing up, Terrance frequently asked his parents why his grandparents never came to visit them, why every holiday trip was from Denver to Wichita and never the other way. His mother, Faith Newell, the eldest of three daughters—who often complained herself that her parents never visited—always blamed their living on a farm as the root of her parents' unwillingness to travel.

"There are a lot of responsibilities you have on a working farm, son," Faith said. "When it comes to feeding livestock and milking cows, there is no such thing as a holiday."

By the time Terrance was a teenager, his grandparents Burt and Darla had sold off virtually all their livestock and Burt proudly told anyone who asked—and quite a few who didn't ask—that they were retired. When Terrance asked why his grandparents never traveled to visit them now that they were retired, his mother would reply, "I guess they're just set in their ways."

Burt Watkins eventually died, leaving his wife alone in an ample farmhouse. Since Darla had no transportation (she was of that generation that believed it was a luxury and unnecessary for a woman to learn to drive), Faith—who was now a divorced, middle-aged professional woman—decided she should move back to Wichita and care for her mother. This was despite the fact that Edith and Regina, her two younger sisters, lived in close proximity to Darla, as did many of their children. After this transition, when Terrance asked why his mother did not bring his grandmother to Denver to visit him, she would say, "Son, I'm just so busy with my work, trying to get re-established and everything. Plus, your grandmother really doesn't like to travel."

"How do you or Gram know that," Terrance asked, "seeing how she has never traveled anywhere?"

"Are you still dating that girl in your accounting department?" Faith asked, adroitly changing the subject so as to put Terrance on the defensive.

For his part, Terrance had long since quit believing that his grandmother remained at home out of personal choice. When he was a child, Grandma Darla often spoke to him and his cousins about the exciting places in the world she had read about in Readers Digest Condensed books and seen on television. Burt, his blustery grandfather, was the one who never wanted to leave the proximity of Wichita. Dutiful wife that she was, Darla would never think of challenging him. Terrance couldn't help but note that his mother, Faith, was a lot more like his grandfather than were either of his two aunts. Both Edith and Regina, like Darla, were soft-spoken, never asserting themselves, living out the same sort of submissive, receding lifestyle that their mother embodied—even though they did occasionally travel out of the state of Kansas.

It dawned on Terrance one day that he had only asked his mother why Grandma Darla never traveled to see him. Why didn't he ask Darla herself?

When he called her, he had in mind a carefully planned approach. First he asked how things were going on the farm ("same as always") and how things were going with his aunts, his cousins and finally his mother ("good; she works too hard, I think, but she's just fine"). When Darla grew restive of his asking her about her uneventful life, she asked him—just as he had anticipated—what was new in his life. He began to talk about the wonderful cultural life of Denver and the magnificence of the Rockies. In particular, he said, he was anticipating the beauty of springtime that was going to descend on his city in only a few weeks. "I know how much you like gardens, Grandma. You should come and see how special this place is after winter is over and the weather is mild."

"Oh, I only wish I could, Terry."

"Why don't you, Gram?"

"Oh, I'm sure you mother couldn't get the time off to take me."

"She's kind of her own boss, Gram. You and I know she can

take off all the time she needs."

"Well, she would have to set aside some of her work, which would be inconvenient and probably cost her some money. And I just know she wouldn't let me pay for the gas money to drive all that way."

"Okay, but if she agrees to bring you, you'd come to Denver, right?"

Darla hesitated, clearly alarmed that her grandson was not being dissuaded. "Well, I—"

"It's settled, then," Terrance said triumphantly. "I'll give Mom a call and let her know what we've decided." Then he got off the phone without letting his grandmother say any more about the proposed trip.

Terrance was under no illusions that his mother was going to agree to drive his grandmother to see him—or that Darla would acquiesce and ride along if she did. He knew that the hard part was still ahead. It was with a playfully irreverent attitude he immediately called up his mom.

"Mom, I've got great news. At long last Grandma has agreed to let you bring her to Denver."

Faith was stunned. "You asked your grandmother?"

"Of course. That's okay, isn't it?"

"Well, yes, but—"

"But what?"

"Well, your grandmother is such a homebody. I can just see me arranging to take the time off and at the last minute she backs out and refuses to go."

"Has she ever done that before?"

"Well, no, but—"

"And don't you set your own schedule? You two just tell me when it's convenient for you to come and I'll be ready for you."

"Well, we'd have to get a hotel room. You can't put us up in your apartment."

"Why not? I have three bedrooms and usually I only sleep in one."

This was the first salvo of the "Trip Wars," characterized by Faith working diligently to find a "logical" reason—that is, one that Terrance would accept as valid—for her not to drive her mother to Denver, while Terrance successively and successfully *found ways to parry her excuses. The skirmishes were conducted over the phone, in a series of letters and through third-party conversations. Terrance took to calling his mild-mannered aunts, calmly expressing vexation with his mother and wondering aloud why she was trying to prevent Grandma Darla from taking a simple trip for the first time in her life. Of course, Terrance knew, and intended, that every word he said was being repeated to Faith and Darla. He also knew that the level of anxiety among the older women in his family was ballooning as he refused to let go of the issue, also as he intended.*

Grandma Darla tried to defuse the conflict by backing out of the trip—which, after all, she had never agreed to in the first place. Terrance played it off by telling her he knew she really did want to see Denver in springtime and that she shouldn't let her daughter ruin her plans just because Faith was such a stick-in-the-mud who had gotten to where she didn't want to travel. He sent his grandmother color brochures about the various gardens, vistas and springtime attractions that beckoned, included with schedules of where they could go at what time on various days of the week. He made sure to include chatty letters, playing up his intended hospitality and invariably closing with words to the effect, "Now remember, Gram, this is just between you and me," to make sure his grandmother would anxiously share them either with his mother or with one of his aunts who would quickly tell his mother.

Faith grew increasingly frustrated and angry. For the first time in Terrance's memory, his mother stopped answering the phone immediately when she saw it was him calling. He responded by leaving her lengthy, very cheerful voicemails, describing how much he was looking forward to her visit. Faith eventually called Terrance and told him to drop the whole business, that his grandmother did not want to visit Denver and that, as Darla's daughter and his mother, she was ashamed of his roiling the family with this ridiculous idea. At that point, he calmly followed through with the next step of his plan.

"That's just you talking, Mom. I don't know why you're afraid of letting Gram see a tiny, little snippet of the civilized world; but frankly I'm tired of waiting for you to get with the program, so I've decided to take matters into my own hands."

Faith paused, curious and furious at the same time. "Just what do you think you're going to do?"

"You're not interested in our trip, so does it matter?" Taking a page from his mother's book, he changed the subject. "I've been meaning to ask you, Mom, are you still going on that business trip to Seattle this summer?"

The next day he called Aunt Regina and asked her what his grandmother's schedule was for the upcoming weekend. He said he wanted to surprise Darla and finalize plans for her trip to Denver.

Regina was stunned. "But . . . your mother told me they weren't going."

"Oh, Mom's not coming. I'm going to make arrangements to bring Gram here myself."

". . . Well, are you going to work this out with your mom?"

"Mom? Oh, I'm not planning to see her this weekend at all."

Regina gasped. "You're coming to Wichita, but you're not going to see your mom."

"Oh I talk to her all the time," he said casually. "It's really no big deal."

Terrance knew that, before the hour was over, his grandmother, mother and aunts would have had several conversations about his weekend excursion to Wichita. What he did not know was whether or not his mother could contact him in a rage. When he didn't hear from her, he assumed she was waiting to find out if he really intended to travel all the way from Denver to Wichita and not see his mother—which was precisely what he did.

As Terrance anticipated, his grandmother didn't seem too surprised when he showed up on her doorstep just before lunchtime on Saturday. In fact, she had a nice lunch prepared and the two enjoyed a most pleasant chat. Afterward Terrance produced his tablet computer and gave her a little visual preview of the places he intended to take her to in Denver. She was clearly touched by the great gesture of his coming to see her, not to mention quite curious about the images he showed her; it reminded him a little of the excitement she had shown in distant places when he was a child. Half-heartedly she went through her familiar list of reasons she shouldn't make the trip. Terrance didn't even bother to brush them aside.

"Are you scared to fly, Gram? If you are, I'll drive you. But it's a long drive for me to come here, drive you there and then drive you back."

"Well, your mother—"

"This doesn't concern Mom, Gram. She has her reasons for opting out. You're coming to visit a place unlike anywhere you've been before."

Darla smiled ruefully. "That's just because I've never really been anywhere before."

"That's right. And this is just the start. There's a whole big world that's just been waiting for you out there." He showed her a calendar. "Now let's pick some dates so I can start pricing flights."

Two days after he got home, Terrance received a letter from his mother. She expressed great disappointment in him for coming to Wichita and not stopping to see her. She said he was being totally irresponsible in expecting a woman his grandmother's age to fly for the first time and even more irresponsible in spending "that much money" on airline tickets. Therefore, Faith said, she had decided to end this ridiculous conflict between them and to drive Darla to Denver on the dates Terrance had set aside for the trip. "I'm not going to forget you've done this, son," her letter concluded.

A grand smile spread across his face. "Yes!"

We'll be coming back to this onerously long story both throughout this chapter and the next, but first, let's focus on the way Terrance defined himself. The amazed dismay expressed by all the significant women in his life when he continued to insist that his grandmother travel to Denver clearly indicates that prior to the Trip Wars, they had perceived Terrance to be a "good boy," dutiful and desirous of pleasing these people he loved. Thus his challenge to Darla's stay-at-home status was viewed as being totally out of character for him. When he made a decision to follow a unique, unpredictable path for the first time, the resistance he met from his family was tremendous. Everyone kept waiting for him to "wake up" and embrace their expectations of him.[xix] During the Trip Wars, Terrance did feel several times that he was being unreasonable; he felt guilty for submitting these folks he loved to the whim of his desire to break up the ritual of "keeping granny home"; he feared he was driving a wedge between himself and his cherished female relatives. The key thing is, he also recognized this was exactly how they wanted him to feel. In fact, the outcome of these Trip Wars was a victory for Terrance as well as for his grandmother because it helped him define himself. As the struggle went on, he felt himself emerging more and more as an individual with greater freedom. Clearly, he recognized, he had acquired a powerful position within his family he had never assumed before: never assumed as in "did not expect he could have" and never assumed as in stepping into a new role ("the mayor assumed his duties").

The first characteristic to work on acquiring, then, is a clearer definition of who you are as a person, a clearer idea of what the family expects of you and of how you are going to react to that. I hope it's obvious that I'm not saying you should suddenly become a rebel who turns your family upside down. Rather I'm saying that you should get to know yourself, what truly motivates you as a person and how much courage and willingness you possess when it comes to renewing your family. I encourage you to get to know yourself as well as you're getting to know your kinfolks, their motives and their stuckness.

For the remainder of this chapter, we will take a look at some other characteristics you'll find helpful as you make and fulfill your plans to fix your family. Working on acquiring these qualities will increase your ability to be well-defined. Simultaneously, the better defined you are, the easier it will be to develop these traits. Not too many of us naturally possess these characteristics. By the same token, I've never encountered anyone who wanted to acquire and use these qualities who wasn't able to do so to the sufficient degree necessary to challenge personal and family stuckness. Again, these are characteristics you can understand right away and acquire over time with practice—and your family will give you plenty of opportunities for that.

You First

The next quality to discuss is the **willingness to step into a leadership role** in your family. Every family has a leader or leaders. Sometimes changing, challenging situations cause different individuals to emerge as family leaders. In your case, you could say that—if you aren't already the significant leader of your clan—the stuckness in the family is the circumstance that caused you to come forth as a leader.

If you go back to your family gram and look at each generation you charted, you should be able to tell pretty easily exactly who was/is calling the shots. If your family is mired in stuckness, that implies someone was/is leading them to be stuck—and yes, that can be you; and yes, you can change it. Consider that family life itself is a journey and someone is leading the family on a particular pathway. If that path is unproductive and unpleasant, if that path is not conducive to the personal growth and well-being of the various members of the family, then it's time to choose a new path. The emergence of a new family path is sometimes unintentional,[xx] but real changes don't have to be left to chance. Indeed, if you're waiting for your family to get better on its own, you may be waiting for generations. Stuckness inhibits healing. If, on the other hand, the right person emerges and challenges the perpetually unrewarding pathway the family has been following, the entire family can be transformed.

It's important to recognize, I think, that the "change agent," the emerging leader, does not have to know exactly how she or he wants things to be; that is, you don't have to know all the twists and turns of the new pathway your family will take. Your job is to help the family get unstuck. When it happens, new directions, new power, new freedom, new insight, new hope and new joy often spontaneously erupt within the family. And the family itself will chart a new pathway. It's helpful to remember here that *healing is a natural process*. If you remove that which is keeping the family stuck in a repetitive cycle, the family can find its own way forward—which, by the way, is a beautiful thing to watch. Once you have helped to accomplish this, you will find your position in the family enhanced. You will be recognized as a true leader (when they need someone to lead, they likely will come back to you).

There is one more extremely important factor you need to recognize about being a leader in your family: regardless of the group you're leading, *leaders are lightning rods for criticism*. So when you are guiding your family (or any group) in the direction you perceive to be proper and best, you should anticipate you will be criticized. Please know that the criticism you will receive will hurt you and you will question yourself. In light of this, therefore, I'm going to tell you one mighty truth that will empower you to keep on leading even when you're being dope-slapped by people who should be supporting you. Ready? *Criticism is a form of pursuit.* Got it? Criticism is a form of pursuit.[xxi]

All this time, as you have been enduring a multitude of critical comments, you have been thinking that criticism is a form of disapproval, or criticism is a form of scorn or criticism is a form of disconnection. It may be all those things, but whatever else it is—and most importantly—criticism is a form of pursuit. Back in the day when I held regular seminars for leaders of congregations, I used to tell them they should go find a tattoo parlor and have "Criticism is a form of pursuit" inked backwards on their chests just below their throats so they would read it every morning as soon as they looked in the mirror. I would also tell these leaders that the degree of criticism they were receiving was in fact an indication of the degree to which they were being pursued; that is, *if the criticism you are receiving is out of proportion to the criticism you deserve (and we all deserve a little), then either you have something or you are something that your critic greatly desires.*[xxii] Several good things can come from this awareness. For one thing, you can quit taking the criticism personally; frankly it's sort of a left-handed compliment. For another, you begin to realize that the real problem isn't so much what they are criticizing you for as it is the personal need of the critic. And for a third, the best way to handle unwarranted criticism is to move toward the critic emotionally (see the section below on being connected).

How did this dynamic play itself out in our example of Terrance and his family? Well, who was the leader before Terrance initiated the Trip Wars? The leader for many decades was the patriarch of the family, Burt Watkins. Clearly, he had instituted the "stay-at-home" policy in which his wife Darla had become mired. After his death, his firstborn child, Faith, stepped into the role and perpetuated the practice of keeping Darla at home; this policy "just felt right" to everyone in the family, even if everyone in the clan sometimes lamented publicly or privately what a shame it was that Darla never went anywhere.

It's also clear that Terrance stepped into a leadership role—not

Faith's role, but a different leadership role—when he began his struggle to free Darla from the farm. I think it's important to note that all he had to do to emerge as a leader in the family was to ask the right questions and to not settle for the disinformation everyone had been accepting for decades. This was no "regime change." Terrance had no desire to step into his mother's new role as family leader, and indeed he did not. Nonetheless, he did make a new, substantial place for himself that did not undermine but rather strengthened the family. You might note as well that, as the conflict continued, Faith became very critical of her son. Even when she submitted to his desire to bring Darla to see him, she criticized him. Terrance recognized it for what it was: his mother was submitting, but not surrendering; this allowed her to remain the de facto leader of the family, but also allowed Terrance to assert a leadership role as well, which worked to everyone's benefit.

This May Take a While

Another characteristic to be cultivated by those who want to fix their families is a sort of dual capability: **patience** and **persistence**. One way to define stuckness in a family is, "chronic inability to deal with a past emotional trauma or circumstances." That is, stuckness is something that develops and "hardens" over time and—contrary to the promises of motivational speakers who proclaim they can permanently remove bad habits and corrupt self-image instantaneously—fixing family stuckness takes time.[xxiii] Changing perverse family traditions (by the way, "perverse family traditions" might be another good definition for stuckness) requires the ability to stay with the process in the face of resistance.

I've long appreciated a proverb about persistence that, I was told, originated with Winston Churchill: "The bulldog's nose is slanted backwards so it can breathe without letting go."

Begging the pardon of Sir Winston, I'd like to build on this wonderful metaphor he used to describe the value and necessity of persistence. Consider the difference between the English Bulldog, the Chihuahua and the Rottweiler. The Chihuahua is essentially an annoying "early warning system." Its function is to let people know that something unusual and perhaps threatening is going on.

Dr. Mike Simpson

The Rottweiler is an attacker. Its function is to destroy things so that whatever might have been a threat can no longer threaten. The English Bulldog, on the other hand, is a persuader. The bulldog grabs hold and hangs on until whomever it has hold of decides to become nonthreatening. As a change agent in your family, you'll find more success if you don't annoy people with your yipping about how things are wrong, if you don't break down the family even more with harsh attacks, but rather if you just grab hold of folks where it's uncomfortable and hang on until they're ready to listen.

Hand in hand with persistence is patience. Patience, you may find, is not only a virtue but also a weapon. We've all dealt with businesses, bureaucracies and websites whose real intent is to dissuade you from achieving what you are trying to do by making the process impenetrably complex and time-consuming. Nothing is more unnerving to those who practice such passive-aggressive behavior than a person who is willing to patiently, cheerfully wait and comply. When people put your patience to the test, you might try to hold the thought, "Let's see if they can really outlast me." And remember, the longer *you* wait without becoming angry, the harder it is on *them*.

A colleague of mine was once asked to take on a particularly difficult task within our non-profit co-op. He wavered at the time he was asked; he didn't want the job, even though he and everyone else in the outfit knew he was the right person for it. Ultimately, I was put in the position of getting an answer out of him. I knew if I were demanding and made him angry, that would give him the emotional impetus to say "no." Somehow I had to "corner him" so he would have to give the obvious response. For several days I called his office and sent him emails, trying to schedule any kind of a meeting. Then an idea hit me. I went to my office assistant and asked her to call this fellow's office assistant, a woman she knew pretty well.

"Now, Betty," I said, "you know that Sally keeps Dr. Felton's appointment book. I want you to get her to schedule me in for his first available lunch. She is going to try to avoid doing that, but I don't want you to let her off the phone until we have a lunch date set."

"What if she hangs up on me?"

"She's not going to do that. Just keep being pleasant and chatty, but under no circumstance hang up until you've gotten the appointment."

I sat beside her desk as Betty made the call. She was a natural. She must've visited with Sally for two or three minutes before bringing up the lunch engagement—even though Sally surely knew the purpose of the call from the beginning. True to form, Sally tried several times and ways to get Betty off the phone, but—with a grin on her face—Betty refused to hang up, cheerfully suggesting dates for the lunch appointment. Eventually Sally put Betty on hold. I realized that Dr. Felton was sitting beside his administrator's desk, just as I was sitting beside mine.

"Now what?" Betty asked.

"Now she'd going to come back on and suggest a date."

Thirty seconds later, Dr. Felton and I had our luncheon scheduled.

And what about Terrance? Given that this struggle played itself out over the course of about six weeks, he was a true paragon of persistence and patience during the Trip Wars. I think it's important to note that, throughout the ordeal, apart from his grandmother's interest in the photos and schedules he showed her, he received no encouragement whatever until the moment his mother cratered and agreed to deliver Darla to Denver. Opening doors that have long been closed requires persistence and patience. . . . "Deliver Darla to Denver"; that could be, like, a country song.

You Saw That Coming, Right?

The next important characteristic to work on developing is the **ability to anticipate** the reactions and decisions of your family members as you confront the stuckness within it. As a teenager, you pretty much knew the answer to all the requests you were making of your parents before you ever asked; you know how everybody in your family will vote in any given election; you know how certain people should be discouraged from sitting by certain other people if everyone is to enjoy Thanksgiving dinner. It's important to remember you do still possess this ability and you are wise to put it to use as you make a plan to unstick your family.

As you begin to emerge as a change agent, it's a good idea to ask yourself who in your family will be your ally? Who will resist you? How will they resist you (momentarily we're going to delve into the various types of resistance)? What allowances will you have to make for the predictable responses you're going to get?

One of the most amazing phenomena I've witnessed over the years is the sight of bright, well-prepared, logical people trying to convince a particular group of people of which they are a part to make a certain decision, only to fail miserably—then not have a clue as to why their plan didn't succeed. Invariably these good people make the same mistake: they rely on logical reasoning and believe that their clear, rational presentations will inevitably sway anyone who has doubts about the efficacy of their plans.[xxiv] They regularly fail because—harkening back to the very first observation we made in Chapter One—human beings are not rational; they are emotional. It's all well and good to have logical reasons for the plans we set forward, but *the best-laid plans of mice, men and women will inevitably go astray if the emotional processes of the group are not made the priority of the change agent.*

Let's talk for a moment about resistance. Perhaps you've heard the proverb, "No good deed goes unpunished." Since, by definition, unsticking your family and empowering them to live out their shared journey with new power and freedom is not just a good deed but an outstandingly excellent deed, you can anticipate somebody in the family will fight you tooth and toenail to prevent your achieving the change you seek. Even as they do this, they will assume they are upholding what is right, proper and worthy and that you are trying to bring degradation down upon your family. I think it's important to remember that what they are feeling is not evil and, since it's purely emotional rather than logical, we could not call it being "short-sighted"; short-sightedness implies vision and, by definition, emotions impede vision—or at least they force one's vision as if looking through a tunnel. In reality, those opposing you are basically attempting to maintain the emotional balance of the family. In order to succeed, you have to shift or tip that emotional balance. Thus they aren't so crazy, are they? They're just stuck and need someone to help them get unstuck, even as they do their best to prevent it.

I don't mean to make this resistance sound so impermeable that change is impossible. The underlying emotional reality (and I understand, yes, this sounds perverse) is that, to a certain degree in an uncanny way, those resisting you simultaneously hope you succeed. Like I said, this sounds perverse and it's counter-intuitive, but it's also a dependable truth. I think this is because, on some level, the family knows it has to have creative leadership, which is what you represent. Ed Friedman would probably say the family is testing you to determine your worthiness to lead. Ed was also fond of pointing out that the great European explorers of the sixteen and seventeenth centuries all faced and overcame shipboard mutinies.

Your wonderful family members will have three distinct methods of resisting you. The first, most basic and obvious is the direct attack or what we can call **negation** or **opposition**. This simply means that *when you say you want to do something, others in the family will say, "No, we aren't going to do that."*

I remember a newly-elected American President proposing a sweeping plan that would be of great and obvious benefit to millions of the citizens of our nation. No sooner had the President announced an intent to begin this new program than the Senate leader of the opposite party, when asked for his response, replied, "Where's he going to get the money?" Note that the senator did not bring up the worthiness or the necessity of the new program, he just negated the possibility that his party would support it. Opposition is the simplest, clearest, most honest form of resistance. In its way, it's the easiest to endure and overcome.

In our vignette, Terrance encountered powerful opposition from his mother. Faith offered a series of reasons why Darla could not travel to Denver for a visit with her grandson. None of her objections were difficult to argue against or stood up to reason very well. Why? Of course, because Faith's opposition was primarily emotional. One of the frequent characteristics of the arguments made by opponents to change is that their arguments, when carefully examined, tend not to stand up to reason. By the same token, you can't "make them see reason" such that opponents change their minds. Rather, you have to deal with their emotions surrounding the issue—something we're going to discuss fully in the next chapter.

A second common and somewhat thornier form of resistance is what we call **sabotage**. For our purposes, we will define sabotage as when those who are supposed to be supporting your efforts in fact take steps to undermine them; or even simpler, *sabotage is when you are torpedoed by people who are supposed to be on your side.*

Ever try to plan a surprise party and someone in the family "lets the cat out of the bag" so the person who was to be surprised finds out about it? That's sabotage. Ever have someone suddenly develop a huge personal problem or cause a massive mess just when you need to be concentrating on an important family issue? Ever find yourself in the midst of carrying out some plans that mean a great deal to you (the classic example is when you ask someone in your family to carry the cake/punch bowl/chip-and-dip tray across the room to the serving table and that person drops it)? That's sabotage. Ever trust someone in your family with an important secret and they manage to tell the one person whom you didn't want to know? That's sabotage.

Sabotage often develops when the level of stress/anxiety in a family system rises to a point beyond what certain folks in the family can bear. As you think about the different units in your family just now, you probably have a good idea of who can handle stress better than whom. Think about the "distractor" in your family who manages to say the inappropriate thing, calling attention to himself or herself and away from whatever the family is dealing with at the moment. When a leader (that's you) is attempting a creative new way of dealing with a family problem and gets sabotaged, that sabotage is actually an uncanny attempt at restoring the family's emotional balance.

Perhaps you are familiar with the Yiddish concept of the *shlemiel* and the *shlimazel*. The *shlemiel* is a chronically clumsy, inept, destructive person who constantly breaks things and disrupts whatever group she/he is in. The *shlimazel* is the person who is most often the victim of the *shlemiel's* actions. A Yiddish aphorism describes it this way: "A *shlemiel* is somebody who often spills his soup; a *shlimazel* is the person on whom the soup lands." For our purposes, let's describe the *shlemiel* as a sort of family saboteur who is intent on disrupting your efforts to bring about change within the family's emotional processes. After all, if I can mock you, get you to be emotional and distract others from the importance of the moment, I've done great harm to your intention of shifting the family's emotional processes. Your task, as a change agent, is not to allow yourself to become the *shlimazel*. When, in the middle of a family discussion, the family klutz breaks a crystal serving dish that was precious to you, you have to be prepared for how to deal with it without being deterred from your intent: "Bob, if you didn't bring your checkbook, we'll have to discuss another form of payment. Now where was I?"

I think it's important to note that saboteurs are often not intentional about the disruption they cause. Many times they really do believe they are on your side, even as they are doing everything they can to shoot down your plans. We see this dynamic all the time, don't we, with people who are described as being "their own worst enemies." The diabetic sabotages herself by inadvertently strolling past the donut shop; the workaholic, having pledged to take the weekend off, realizes he has forgotten to respond to that one business email. On an intellectual level, we make decisions and stick to them; our emotions, however, are impervious to logic. Thus, when you are seeking help in your efforts to unstick your family, you have to ask, "Who can I trust to handle the pressure of what we're doing without stabbing me in the back?"

In reflecting on our reference story, you might say, "Well, lucky for Terrance, he didn't encounter any sabotage. Ah, but he did. It came from the source that was most difficult for him to bear: his grandmother. While Darla was clearly interested in what a trip to the exotic locale of Denver might hold for her, rather than working with Terrance to make the trip happen, she consistently tried to discourage her grandson and took the side of Faith throughout the Trip Wars. Further, whenever Terrance discussed possible plans for the trip, Darla promptly related all this information to Faith. For his part, Terrance knew he could not count on his grandmother to step up and proclaim a willingness to take the trip. If she had, he knew, his mother would have talked her out of it. *Fixing* your family requires *dealing* with your family and that implies *recognizing* who is capable of sincerely helping you and who might undermine your efforts.

The third form of resistance is the subtlest and sometimes the most difficult to overcome. We call it **embrace and fuse** and I would define it as *the stuck family enveloping the would-be change agent with extraneous distractions and responsibilities so that* *he/she cannot proceed with the desired changes.* To use a simple illustration, let's say Grandma Janice wants to spend more time with her two granddaughters. Let's say she has become convinced that Loretta, her daughter-in-law, is way too much of a "helicopter mom" who hovers over the girls and the two tweens need to have more of an exposure to the exciting possibilities of the world than they are receiving. Janice asks Loretta for permission to take the girls on a week-long beach and shopping trip to buy them clothes for the upcoming school year. Janice is surprised and delighted when Loretta agrees. As time for the trip gets closer, Loretta begins to produce lists of things Janice must do for the girls during the trip: allergy medication schedules, ambient noise sources for sleeping, menu requirements (who knew the girls had to stay away from gluten, carbs, sugar and all nut products), sunblock (SPF #15 simply will not offer enough protection) and so on. Just a day or two before the trip—about which Janice is decidedly less enthusiastic—Loretta announces that the girls will not be available on the agreed-upon date, but will have to leave for the trip a day later than promised; one of them has a dental appointment (how lucky that an appointment with this highly-recommended doctor suddenly became available). Then Loretta asks if they can come home half a day earlier because one of the children needs to practice for her dance recital. As she hangs up the phone after the last call, Janice is near tears. "This isn't a glorious week of new experiences for the girls," she exclaims, "this is really just a few days of me living out Loretta's agenda!"

If you read the endnotes, you may have seen the quote from my friend who said she had learned as a child "people tell you that you are being good when you're doing what they want you to do." If your family is stuck and you regularly find yourself fulfilling the desires of other family members, chances are you are not only *not* a change agent, not a leader, but you are perpetuating the stuckness in the family even as you make others happy. If you want to fix your family, you will probably have to overcome the temptation to please them—particularly when they ask you to set aside your own agenda in favor of theirs or of the conventional "family tradition."

In our example in this chapter, Terrance did not encounter *embrace and fuse* resistance. If you, however, are recognized in your family as a dutiful, caregiving member, then chances are you will be sucked in and expected to fulfill the traditional family agendas of others. And if you decide to become an agent of change, you can be certain that family members will come up with important responsibilities with which to distract you from the changes you want to institute.[xxv]

This Is Too Important to Take Seriously
I don't know what your experience is, but I find that the mere discussion of resistance in all its forms tends to leave me feeling frustrated and maybe a little angry. Therefore it's fitting that we move to a discussion of an antidote to anger, frustration and anxiety: **playfulness**. As unlikely and childlike as it might seem, maintaining a playful attitude is an extremely important quality to develop for those who desire to make change in their families a reality.

And by the same token, a key attitude to avoid is **seriousness**. Ed Friedman famously, constantly warned his Emotional Process students, "Don't let them 'serious you up.'" If you think about your experiences within your family, chances are that the more stuck your family is, the more likely everyone's attitude is either serious or resigned to despair or both. And, if I don't miss my guess, the main purveyors of stuckness are the main purveyors of seriousness . . . or maybe it's the other way around.

Marlene was one of the folks we worked with for whom playfulness came in quite handy and gave her some newfound ability to assert herself within her marriage. Her husband, Griff, tended to be extremely detached. He was scarcely involved in their home life, leaving child rearing, housekeeping, event planning and other "mundane" tasks to his wife. When it came to things he was interested in, however, he demanded that he get his way. Marlene perceived Griff to be her intellectual superior, and there was a sort of drama that played itself out whenever she would ask him to assist with the family to any extent or she would seek his help with a specific task in which he had no interest. Marlene would get flustered and tongue-tied as the argument progressed. Griff would begin to mock her, correcting her sentence construction, word choices and using his own convoluted logic to turn her thinking on its head. Totally discouraged, Marlene would surrender in despair, and Griff would retreat to the sofa with the TV remote and a smirk of victory.

To counter this script, we pointed out to Marlene that Griff wasn't dealing with the issue she wanted to address, but rather was intentionally distracting her. We coached her not to let Griff change the subject and, above all, not to fall for his ability to make her anxious about what she perceived as her deficiencies. His tendency to compare intellects, as we pointed out, was a red herring—not a real concern. Actually, Griff being a consummate slacker was the only pertinent issue. To overcome his routine, we said, she needed to remain playful and not allow Griff to get her anxious or serious.

Because Griff was not easily going to give up his ritual of cleverly berating her, Marlene knew she needed to create and rehearse a series of responses to him that were demure, charming and playful—all qualities Marlene possessed to a much, much greater extent than Griff had or had the ability to resist. So, when she asked him to get off the couch and put the kids to bed or help in other ways and he tried to confound her by pointing out the imperfections in the way she had asked, she was ready:

"Honey, I feel so sorry for you every day, being married to an intellectual inferior and still having to put her kids to bed." Or, "I know what you're saying, Griff. You'd have been so much better matched if you'd married an English teacher, who had a housekeeper." Or, "Oh, sweetheart, I'm too stupid to reach the crockpot. Could you be smart and reach it for me?"

In our tale of the Trip Wars, we can see that Terrance remained playful throughout the entire conflict, even as most others in the family became quite serious. His mother, aunts and grandmother got to the point of viewing his behavior with alarm, which by definition ratcheted up the degree of anxious seriousness exponentially. For his part, Terrance anticipated the stress these beloved family members would be feeling and knew that remaining playful would tend to relieve a great deal of the anxiety throughout the process. *Harmless playfulness is a wonderful tool that allows the change agent to remain focused and persistent without coming across to others in the family as being threatening.*

There are a couple of notes I'd like to emphasize here about being playful. First, as Ed Friedman said in *Generation to*

Generation, being playful does not mean you have to "zing people with one-liners." To be sure, humor is a wonderful way to express playfulness—though not the only way. Playfulness is an attitude that you can adopt, whereas the ability to be humorous in a given, tense situation may escape us. I would observe, however, that the more you practice being playful, the easier it will be to be humorous as well.

Second, we can't always be playful. Faith wrote some pretty harsh things to her son; and Terrance had his moments when he had to relax, clear his head and plan his response so he wouldn't come back in a hostile, serious way. If you can't be playful in a given moment, call a little "emotional timeout," relax, and be good to yourself for a while. Playfulness is resilient; she will return to you.

And in this vein, I encourage you not to try to be humorous when you are not able to feel lighthearted and playful. If you are angry or hurt or grieving, attempts at humor will come out sounding like snarky cynicism. I know this from my own experience. A day or so after the death of Ed Friedman, at a time when I was feeling bitter grief (after all, the guy didn't ask me if he could die), I went into a church board meeting and asked the group to approve a large purchase. Those opposing the purchase had, in my view, a very weak case and I meant to tease them about it playfully. Unfortunately for all of us, my words came out full of mockery and scorn. The purchase was voted down. Six months later, after I had done some groundwork with the board and made a funny, somewhat irreverent presentation, the same purchase was approved without opposition.

That Is Exactly Not What I Meant

Probably you aren't old enough to remember this; but back before electricity when we had to watch TV by candlelight, there was a comedy program called *All in the Family*. The star of the show was one of the dumber heroes of American television: Archie Bunker. One of the constant ironies of the show was that willfully ignorant Archie continually referred to his graduate student son-in-law Mike as "meathead." I mention Bunker's intellectual depth in part because one's degree of intelligence doesn't necessarily have much to do with one's ability to use

Emotional Process to achieve one's goals. In one episode the Bunkers decide to go on a trip. At the moment of their departure, a girl of about ten or eleven who was living with them announces that she isn't going (the program had a way of being a little too realistic sometimes). Rather than demanding, begging or cajoling, Archie says, "Okay. You can stay here by yourself if you want." He calmly gives the girl a series of rational, believable directions; and then, as he and his wife Edith walk out the door, he says to the child, "You know that door upstairs at the end of the hall? Whatever you do, don't open that door." Archie and Edith step out onto the front porch, and he begins to count. Before he gets to ten, the front door bursts open and the little girl flies past them, ready to accompany them on the trip.

Of course, Archie had no intention of letting her stay by herself, but he knew there was a better way of confronting her absurd behavior than arguing with her about it.[xxvi] Instead he resorted to a sort of misdirection tactic: saying something that is directly counter to the speaker's actual intent. Rather than saying the obvious, "You're too young to stay here by yourself, and we're not going to let you disrupt our plans," Archie was perceptive enough to imply something that showed the child the emotional impact of her staying by herself, "You can stay by yourself if you want to; but if the monster gets out of that room and eats you, we're not responsible." What would you call that tactic? It's sort of like what people used to refer to as "reverse psychology." When I first began to study Emotional Process, I referred to it as "pushing people in the direction they want to go," the idea being that encouraging people to follow through with their own goofy directions and decisions would make them open to more workable solutions to their problems. In the Bowen Theory literature, this tactic is referred to as **paradoxical intent** or simply **a reversal**: *making an observation or suggestion that is counter to the speaker's actual intent so as to cause the listener to become clearly aware of the circumstances before them.*

Often when families would come to Ed Friedman to work on their issues and they would pour out examples of why, no matter how hard they worked on their troubles, they just couldn't make any progress, he would suggest, "Well what if you just tried harder?" This invariably provoked an incredulous response of dismay. Of course, Friedman knew that trying harder would only perpetuate the difficulties they were struggling with. By suggesting it—the reverse of his intent—he put them in the position of recognizing the futility of what they had been trying and as a result, they became much more open to whatever he was going to suggest.

Probably the most famous example of the reversal is a story told about Dr. Murray Bowen from the days when he hospitalized whole families in his attempt to formulate the principles of Family Systems. A middle-aged woman approached him in the hallway of the hospital and asked him for a prescription for a powerful narcotic drug.

"Why do you need that?" Bowen asked.

"Because I'm going to check myself out of the hospital, go home with the pills and kill myself."

Bowen nodded. "And how many pills do you think you'll need for that?" he asked, calmly taking out his pad and writing the prescription.

I've heard several different accounts of what the woman did after that, but the bottom line with each is that she showed back up the next day, ready to work on her family issues. Personally, I would never have had the confidence to make so grand a reversal as Bowen did, but I think he pulled that off in large measure because he knew this woman very well and understood her issues. His paradoxical intent put her in the position of being responsible for her own behavior—pushed her in the direction she insisted she wanted to go. The inevitable result was that she had to deal with and account for the absurdity of her own thinking and actions.

In our Wichita-to-Denver story, Terrance uses paradoxical intent. When he tells his grandmother that his mom, Faith, is out of the picture, he does with the recognition that Faith has no intention of letting anyone other than herself or maybe her sisters take Darla anywhere out of eyesight. And he knows that Darla is going to tell Faith everything he has said. He also knows, when he points out the great distances involved and asks Darla if she would be willing to fly, that neither she nor Faith had any willingness to allow Grandma get on a plane by herself for the first time.

The reversal is most useful when you are able to express it playfully. If you consider that those who are continuing to keep your family stuck are doing so from emotional rather than logical positions, it isn't all that difficult to point out the absurdity of their viewpoints by "pushing them in the direction they want to go."

Stop Me If You've Heard This

Building on the use of playfulness and the reversal, I'd like to encourage you to understand and utilize another important tool that will readily be at your disposal: **gossip**. I'm guessing, of all the concepts I've listed, gossip is probably the one reality that needs no definition or description, although I think it's absolutely essential to point out some little understood and extremely significant truths about gossip.

First, *gossip is a constant reality of life that cannot be completely eliminated.* Second, properly understood, *gossip is an emotional thermometer that will allow you to determine the "emotional temperature" of your family or of any group of which you are a part.* Third, *gossip can be understood as an information pipeline that not only provides you with key information but also allows you to instantly, informally send information throughout the family.*

Gossip and gossips have a notorious, well-deserved reputation for being destructive. One of reasons I hated high school was because of the extremely pernicious "gossip mill" that pervaded the school from which I graduated. In particular, I was aghast as I heard intentional lies being spread about young people, disrupting their lives and destroying relationships. Later, as a young professional, I listened to colleagues pour out their hearts about gossip that tore apart their families and scarred their careers. Thus it took a long time for me to recognize the potential usefulness of gossip. I think the perspective that is most helpful is that gossip is an ever-present reality. It will either be a destructive force or it can be used as a tool of communication to further the agenda of the wise change agent.

Terrance Newell, who had grown up listening to his relatives' continual gossip, had an intuitive grasp of how the process worked. He knew that, by asking the right questions in the proper way, he could find out what was going on within his family of origin at any time. He was able to determine the emotional state of the family through the gossip he overheard and thus was able to determine how much the level of anxiety was increasing. On the one occasion in which he realized he wasn't hearing any gossip—during his trip to Wichita to visit his grandmother but not his mother—Terrance understood that the level of anxiety had reached a high point; he knew that the family was collectively "holding its breath." It was, in fact, this realization that prompted him to wait patiently for a response from his mother, and it turned out to be the very response for which he had been working. We'll come back to this decisive moment below in our discussion of anxiety.

There was one other way Terrance used gossip that is very instructive. I call it the "gossip bomb" (though, of course, nothing actually blows up except the emotional state of the person on the receiving end). If you consider the family gossip mill as a sort of system of pipes and conduits—like the plumbing in a building—Terrance continually "back flushed" the gossip. He recognized that none of his older female relatives (this is not a gender thing; men gossip just as much . . . oh, the stories I could tell) could keep a secret from one another. Thus he understood that whatever he said "in confidence" to one of the aunts or his grandmother would go straight to his mom. When he spoke to Edith or Regina and wondered out loud why his mother was intent on keeping his grandmother stuck on the farm, Terrance knew Faith would hear his comments within the hour.

Accordingly, with your family, it pays dividends to know who can keep a secret and who can't. The ones who are going to blab are therefore useful to you when you need to get a message to someone in the family without coming right out and saying it to them. This is the *gossip bomb: expressing something to someone in a family (or other group) with the recognition that what is said will be passed on to the person for whom the message was actually intended.*

There is another extremely useful and important principle at work here as well. You might ask why Terrance bothered passing his comments about his mother through his aunts and grandmother rather than simply expressing them directly to her. Was he afraid of saying things "to her face"? Well, no. If we consider how much pushback he got throughout the Trip Wars, we have to admit that Terrance wasn't much afraid of saying whatever he needed to say to whomever needed to hear it. Rather, Terrance knew that *we can hear what is said about us far better than we can hear what is said to us.*

Dr. Mike Simpson

When people say things to us directly, we may or may not be very receptive. If we are being criticized, we are almost certain to be defensive, perhaps angry. We put on our emotional hard shells, and only after we hear what that other person has to say do we decide whether or not we are going to be receptive to it. On the other hand, when folks are talking about us, it's as if we are overhearing gossip about our favorite subject—ourselves. And since we don't have to respond (it wasn't said to us anyway) we tend to be more willing to at least consider what is said objectively. When working with families, Ed Friedman frequently said he would say to one person what he wanted another person to hear. Actually it's sort of fun to experiment with this principle to see how it works. If you have adolescents and you are burdened with trying to get them to behave a certain way or "see the light" about a particular issue, you might try turning to that third person in the room—another adult, a sibling, a friend of theirs—and calmly stating what you can't quite get through to the teenager.

Building on this notion, whether you are speaking to the person you want to get through to or allowing that person to overhear what you want to say to her/him, I think your attitude is a key element in getting that person to be receptive. When a spouse wants to convey something of importance to the other spouse, I always coach the speaker to make sure that she/he doesn't try to express this important message during an argument. If you say something of essential importance during a fight, the person to whom you are speaking always has the prerogative to chalk it up as a momentary, hostile statement you didn't actually mean. *If you say something when you are calm and the intended listener is calm, the message and its import has a much better chance of getting through.* This is particularly important when you have an ultimatum to deliver.

I Don't Want You to Worry About This, Okay?

While each of these abilities/characteristics we've described is significant as you work to develop your ability to fix your family, I've intentionally saved the two most important qualities for last. The first of these I want to mention is **the ability to recognize and channel anxiety**. *I would characterize anxiety*—by which I mean nerves, stress, jitters, restlessness, fearfulness, panic, distress, duress, worry, heebie-jeebies and a few dozen other expressions—*as universally destructive*. If you think about the real priority of all troubled families—perpetuating emotional balance—most of the time what families are trying to accomplish by maintaining balance is binding the anxiety they are feeling. Anxiety in a family is like inflammation in the human body: it can definitely harm you and it can't help you. Regardless of the physical issue a patient is dealing with, if inflammation is present, the medical providers have to get it under control before healing can begin; and the worse the inflammation, the more it interrupts the healing process. Just so with anxiety: if you want to fix your family, you must be able to recognize anxiety, and bind it or channel it.

One characteristic of anxiety that makes it very difficult to deal with is its tendency to be *extremely contagious*. You may have witnessed the manner in which one baby in a nursery full of children begins to cry and the other babies either begin to cry or become restless as well. Those tiny babies—not only unable to speak but also unable to comprehend the circumstances that would make another child cry—are simply reacting emotionally to stimuli beyond their intellectual comprehension. Of course, as emotional creatures, we never outgrow the innate tendency to respond to the fearfulness of others with our own fearfulness. As Terrance's behavior caused Faith and Darla to grow more and more anxious, the two aunts also became fretful, despite the fact that neither the son, mother nor grandmother was asking anything of them. Anxiety spreads faster than wildfire.

Among the multitude of things in this world that can elevate the normal, carry-it-around-with-us-everyday level of anxiety we all have (and each of us has a certain degree of worry we bear each day) is change. That's right. *You're trying to bring about change in your family; change increases anxiety; anxiety is a negative force; families resist anything that elevates anxiety; and, therefore, families resist change.* The antidote to this is the leader's willingness and ability to be able to handle and channel anxiety. That is, *if you as the change agent in your family can continue to work for change despite the anxiety you are creating in the family, the family will tend to trust you, thus opening the door for the possibility of change.* And, *if you as the change agent in your family can bind (diminish or limit) the anxiety the family is feeling, your position as a leader in the family will be greatly enhanced.*

So how do you deal with the anxiety you are creating without becoming anxious? We find it helps if you pretend that anxiety is an actual, tangible thing that can be passed from one person to another within the family system. Since I'm assuming that made no sense whatever, let me say it this way: **anxiety is a football or a hot potato**; people will keep trying to pass it to you—especially if you are the person who is brewing it in the family. However, with practice you will find *you can pass the anxiety football off to someone else.* Doing so will invariably provoke an anxious response in them, even as it grants relief to you.

In our Trip Wars tale, Terrance did an excellent job of recognizing the things that provoke anxiety and passing the anxiety off to others when they tried to dump it back on him. When Grandma Darla and Aunt Regina each tried to hand off to him the anxiety he had engendered, Terrance brushed past their objections by saying his mother had made her decision and therefore they should not be concerned about her. He was well aware that he was passing the anxiety football back to Darla and Regina. He also knew that, as their way of channeling the increased anxiety they were feeling, each of them would report his words to Faith. Throughout the Trip Wars, Terrance managed to deflect anxiety back onto his mother. His success in doing so was a big part of the reason Faith ultimately assented to his insistent desire for Darla to come to Denver. Please note (!) that Terrance did not simply dump all the anxiety he could on his mother. Rather this was a gradual process with no malice and—this is essential—he remained connected to her and the other women throughout the implementation of his plan.

On an emotional (preconscious) level, we all recognize anxiety and have an internal method of dealing with it. Babies cry. Some adults talk a lot more when they are anxious. Some talk less. Some get mad and others get giddy. Some get to more and more childlike levels. If you think about the various crises your families have endured, you will be able to determine just how each individual responds to heightened levels of stress, how their roles within the family might change and how easy or difficult it is to relate to them when they are quite anxious as opposed to when they are less anxious.

I would also point out that various members of your family may attempt to use anxiety against you when you are trying to unstick the family system. Rather than viewing this as a personal attack, I think it's important to remember this is something that comes "naturally," an innate method of trying to restore the emotional balance you are disrupting. Remember the way Marlene's husband, Griff, taunted and mocked her speaking ability when she wanted to get him to participate in the life of the family? His haranguing was successful because it increased her anxiety. The more anxious she became, the more she fumbled in her speech and the more Griff was able to criticize her. Marlene found that being playful defused the anxiety Griff was trying to kindle within her (which in turn probably increased his a little; she handed the anxiety football back to him). Also, the simple recognition that someone is trying to make you more anxious—even if it's subconscious on that person's part—often helps to diminish the anxiety you're feeling, the same way that knowing the punch line to a joke or the ending of a suspenseful movie dramatically lessens the tension in the anticipation you feel. And, of course, recognizing that someone is purposefully trying to make you anxious should be an indication to you that you're on target regarding your efforts to unstick your family.

The Single Most Important Quality to Achieve

Legend has it that things were going badly for Napoleon Bonaparte during his attempt to conquer Russia (by the way, *why* did he want to invade Russia?). Mutinous rumblings commenced among his soldiers, with some of them saying aloud that they would kill him if they had the chance. Upon hearing of this, Napoleon jumped on his horse and he rode to the front lines where the grumbling soldiers were bivouacked. They were surprised to see him suddenly appearing among them with no entourage of guards. He dismounted and called out to them, "If any of you wishes to kill his emperor, I am here!" You will not be surprised to hear that the soldiers did not try to kill him but rather prostrated themselves before him in adoration.

What Napoleon achieved in that moment is called **connection**. *Connection is a state of being emotionally present and able to deal calmly with others in your family system.* Being connected does not mean that you totally agree with everyone or that you like, admire, enjoy everyone or even that there is peace and contentment within the group. Connection is a matter of being emotionally present and engaged. Even when Faith, Darla, Edith and Regina totally disagreed with what Terrance was trying to do, he saw to it that he remained emotionally engaged with them; which is to say, *when you are roiling your family with your plans to get them unstuck, it is not only possible but essential that you remain emotionally connected to each person.* To be sure, you may not be able to connect with everyone in your family. Someone may decide you're more of a heretic than he/she can bear. The important thing in such cases is to remain emotionally open, avoid the tendency to become cut off (estranged) and express clearly that the invitation to being connected is available, not as a theoretical possibility but as a legitimate request.[xxvii]

If anxiety is universally bad in relationships, then being connected is universally good in relationships. Please know that I am not intending a theological statement when I affirm that the positive/good always has the ability to overcome the negative/bad, and **the key element that allows the positive to win out is connectedness**. *Seeking and achieving connection washes the anxiety out of individual relationships and out of the system itself.*

This was the final element that helped Terrance succeed in his goal of freeing Darla from the farm. He put a great deal of pressure on his mother in the form of anxiety and through his persistence and playfulness; above all, however, he continued to remain emotionally connected to her. You might ask, "What if Faith had broken the emotional connection between herself and her son?" If she had, it would have been doubly bad. Darla would still be stuck in Wichita, and mother and son would have lost the ability to relate to one another peacefully. Recognizing this, Terrance worked diligently to stay connected.

It is the case that people in your family may decide to break connection with you, or they may decide to refuse your invitation to be connected. In such cases, the first thing to realize is that such decisions are not necessarily permanent. After all, they are emotional decisions and emotions are transient. Sure, some people will judge you to be "bad news" and intellectually decide they will never emotionally "let you in." Again, such decisions are not eternal.

In the next chapter, we'll talk about Friedman's seminal article "The Birthday Party Revisited." In that essay he describes the way his aunt essentially wrote him off and demanded that her offspring have nothing to do with him. At her funeral, he and his cousin's family had a grand time as they got reconnected. Openness to being connected to everyone in your family (and, yes, I had a family member or two myself to whom I didn't especially want to be connected) is the ultimate tool you have and it's the most important one to use in helping your family become unstuck.

When Humphrey Roberts wasn't asked to serve on the church council, he got angry. It wasn't that he came right out and said anything about it. He expressed his anger through the mail. A couple days after the nominating committee sent out the list of prospective church officers in an all-church mailing, Pastor Roy received an envelope from Humphrey containing the list, which had been wadded up, then refolded and mailed back without anything written on it.

The pastor just shook his head. This was vintage Humphrey. Every time an important leadership role was open, Humphrey believed it should be offered to him. There was no position of prestige and authority that Humphrey didn't believe he deserved more than anyone else. Periodically he got passed over for some distinction and he responded by pulling away from the church until someone—usually a minister or the moderator—went to "butter him up" with how essential and important he was to the congregation. Humphrey would solemnly forgive the leadership and say he was man enough to give the church another chance.

Having lived through this ritual several times in the five years of his ministry, Pastor Roy was not surprised when Darrell, the moderator, showed up in his office to say that Humphrey had missed two consecutive Sundays and people were saying was leaving the church.

"Now, Pastor, I think I should tell you that, to anyone who will listen, Humphrey is blaming you for not standing up for him in the nominating committee. He says you must have blackballed him or the committee would have asked him to serve on the council. I guess one of us should go meet with him and ask him please to come back, huh?" Darrell said.

"Let's try something different this time," the pastor said.

Dr. Mike Simpson

"Let's try not begging him to come back. In fact, let's not talk to him at all."

Darrell was shocked. "But what if he doesn't come back?"

"Well I have an idea about how to lure him back," Roy replied, "but it will only work if you and everybody else agrees not to contact him."

The moderator thought it over. "That won't be a problem. Nobody wants to talk to him when he gets like this. What's your plan?"

He shrugged. "I think the church would survive pretty well without Humphrey. What we need to do is show Humphrey how much he needs and misses the church."

The next morning the pastor called the Roberts house. Humphrey answered the phone, as he always did, before the second ring. "Hello."

"Oh, Humphrey," the pastor said, "I was calling for Melany. Is she there?"

Surprised, Humphrey called out for his wife—who was a church volunteer. The minister spoke with her for four or five minutes about a special project he wanted her to work on, making certain in the process not to mention Humphrey.

A couple days later a large, thick manila envelope came in the mail addressed to Melany Roberts. Stamped on the outside, beside the church's return address, were the words, "Privileged and Confidential." Inside the envelope were some documents from one of the women's circles along with a note from the group president asking Melany to call her as soon as she received the envelope to let her know it had arrived safely. A little smile on her face, Melany picked up the phone, right beside Humphrey, and made the phone call.

Saturday evening late, the pastor called again. "Sorry to bother you, Humphrey. Can you tell me whether or not Melany will be in worship tomorrow?"

"Uh. Uh. No. No, we're not coming to—"

"Oh," Roy said, "cutting him off. Well . . . okay. Please tell her I'll just call her next week." He hung up immediately.

Monday morning the pastor received a phone call. It was Humphrey. "We're coming back."

"I beg your pardon?"

"I know you missed us, Pastor, but we were busy the past three Sundays. We'll be back in church this Sunday."

The minister smiled. "Well actually I did miss you, Humphrey, but I assumed if you were gone it was for a good reason. Say, when Melany comes down for her volunteer work this week, could you drop by my office? There are a couple things I wanted to discuss with you."

There are a few lessons to be gleaned from this vignette. I think it's important to note that Pastor Roy never let Humphrey's childish behavior hook him emotionally. Roy could either have given into his fear of losing a long-time, influential member or to his anger at the immature behavior being expressed, particularly regarding the undue criticism. Instead he remembered the great lesson of criticism:[xxviii] because the criticism he received was disproportionate to what he had coming (in point of fact, he didn't deserve any criticism), that meant he had something or he was something Humphrey wanted. While the natural tendency is either to placate or push away someone like Humphrey, the pastor's intention—realizing this parishioner needed the church more than the church needed him—was to find a way to invite Humphrey to pursue him, which worked. By inviting Humphrey to visit him in his study, Roy was reinforcing his connection with him in a way that didn't perpetuate the stuck, humiliating ritual of placating Humphrey and blessing his childish behavior.

We like to say that the sort of behavior Pastor Roy engaged in was a way of *inviting someone to pursue* him. Achieving connectedness in this way—*inviting others to pursue you rather than your pursuing them*—is creative, challenging and fun. Here is a thought experiment for you that will set the stage for you doing the same sort of thing in your family. Who is the most standoffish person in your family; to whom you would like to be a little closer? What do you know about that person's likes/dislikes, relationships, career, personal idiosyncrasies that you could use to open a door through which you could make contact? In what way could you invite that person to make contact with you? When that happens, what will you say in order to maintain a functional, mutual relationship?

And now—you're ready to spark dynamic change in your family!

Key Ideas set forth in Chapter Four: the main concept of this chapter is that there are certain qualities or abilities that we can acquire and develop; to the degree we possess these characteristics, we will find freeing our families from their stuckness to be more achievable. Those qualities are:
- The ability to separate yourself emotionally from other human beings around you—to be *well-defined*—is the first essential quality you'll need to develop as you move toward fixing your family.
- Whether or not you've conceived of yourself as a leader in your family before, the *willingness to step into a leadership role* in your family is key to helping your family become unstuck
- The dual qualities of *patience* and *persistence* are essential dynamics you'll need as you strive to challenge the stuckness of your family.
- Another important characteristic to work on developing is the *ability to anticipate* the reactions and decisions of your family members, particularly resistance to your efforts, as you confront the stuckness within it. We also noted there are three basic types of resistance: *opposition/negation, sabotage* and *embrace and fuse*.
- Maintaining a playful attitude, *playfulness*, is an extremely important quality to develop for those who desire to make change in their families a reality. *Seriousness*, on the other hand, should be avoided in that it tends to maintain the stuckness in the family system.
- Paradoxical intent or the *reversal* is an extremely useful quality for the change agent to acquire; we define it as making an observation or suggestion that is counter to the speaker's actual intent so as to cause the listener to become clearly aware of the circumstances before them.
- Putting *gossip* to use as an emotional thermometer and a channel for receiving and dispensing communication is a key tool for use in working with the stuck family.
- In that *anxiety* in all its forms is a destructive force within

the family, the ability to recognize, bind and channel anxiety is probably the second most important quality of the person desiring to unstick the family.
- If anxiety is the universal bad in relationships, then *connectedness* (achieving and remaining emotional connection) is the universal good in relationships. The ability to achieve and maintain emotional connection with other members of the family is the most important quality a potential change agent can acquire.

Dr. Mike Simpson

5
Arming, Planting and Detonating the Love Bomb

That's Right, I Used the Word "Bomb"
In the creation of this book I wrestled a great deal with how to express certain concepts clearly. I've come to recognize over the thirty plus years in which I've studied and utilized the ideas of Emotional Process that this way of looking at things is not inherently difficult. It is, as I have stated ponderously, a true paradigm shift. It runs completely counter to our shared conventional view of so many human interactions, like therapeutic relationships, leadership, interpersonal communication and so on. We have agonized over expressing things so they are easily understood, yet say precisely what we want them to say. This brings us to "the bomb."

In mid-July, 1991, I was reading Ed Friedman's *Generation to Generation* for the first time. Fortunately there was a dictionary in the room so I could look up some of the words he used that I had not encountered before, or which he used in ways to which I was unaccustomed. He kept using the word "nodal" and talking about "nodal events." After struggling with his use of that word for several hours, I finally figured out that "nodal" was being used as an adjective derived from the word "node," which of course means "a bump." Ed used the term nodal event to describe the noteworthy, milestone experiences of life: weddings, funerals, first jobs, new births and so on. It was clear from what he was saying that nodal events can be any pivotal, life-changing, unforgettable moment in a person's life. For instance, when the sheriff came to tell my grandparents that my uncle's car had been found abandoned on a deserted road, that was a nodal event.

Not just in *Generation to Generation* but in other writings of his, Ed Friedman expressed that *a nodal event can be a planned, intentional occasion, the purpose of which is to attack stuckness in an emotional system.* Ed wrote primarily for clergy and other leaders, but he was quite clear in asserting that the principles he was teaching worked in all groups because all groups form themselves into families. Therefore we can say that, *since it was probably a nodal event of some sort that got your family stuck, a nodal event can initiate the process of unsticking your family as well.*

The problem with explaining this is that crazy expression "nodal event." If you tell somebody you're planning a nodal event, they will have no concept of what you're talking about and wonder what video game or social media platform the idea came from. On the other hand, if you tell someone you're planting a "love bomb," they will be all ears and full of curiosity.

Should I have used the word "bomb?" If there is a universally negative, horrific word, it is "bomb." Sometimes the word is used in colloquial conversation, as when skateboarders glide down a steep hill, they say they have "bombed" it. No one who has seen the ravages of an actual explosive device—large or small—can find anything worthy to say about the word "bomb." My challenge was: I could think of no other adequate expression of what we do when we set about the unsticking of a family. When you plan and succeed in confronting the stuckness in a family, so often it's like an instantaneous, life-changing instant—an explosion. Only it's not evil, bad or destructive. Properly carried off, it's an act of love. What we are learning to do in this chapter is to plan and conduct events that can have the impact of showering compassion, mercy, openness and new vitality throughout your family.[xxix] In addition to describing the process, we're going to use several extended examples to illustrate how love bombs can work, beginning with my own investigations into an event I've been alluding to throughout the book: my father's missing brother, Leslie.

When I told my dad I was going to visit various members of his family in an effort to collect information about the preceding generations of our clan, he immediately expressed a desire to participate. He had no hesitation in driving the 870 miles from his Oklahoma farm to northern Kentucky. I suspected his sudden willingness to help in my research had less to do with curiosity about our family tree than that it presented him an opportunity to play golf with his brothers. Regardless, it fulfilled my intention to meet with him in the place where he grew up.

Dr. Mike Simpson

As is so often the case with such family events, what began as an informal trip involving four or five folks gradually morphed into a mini-reunion, with six of the surviving eleven members of Dad's generation, plus spouses and assorted cousins, gathering for a feast at my Uncle Ronny's house on a Sunday evening. That Sunday morning was devoted to the cemetery tour I wrote about earlier, followed by a trip to the dairy farm where Dad spent most of his youth in a little settlement outside Crittenden, Kentucky. The place was called Heathen Ridge. Dad swore that was its name before the Simpson clan moved there.

The whole idea of formally investigating the family history—though I had not offered Dad any notion of what I was going to do with the information I was gathering—stirred a certain amount of interest among other family units. Thus, when the time came for the Sunday morning excursion, one of my aunts and her daughter asked if they could join us. This suited me perfectly in that their presence prompted Dad to sit in the backseat of the Buick Century I was driving. It was solemnly beautiful to walk through the graveyards and stand before headstones of ancestors who died a hundred years before my birth.

Early in the afternoon when we arrived at the Heathen Ridge farm site, Dad became increasingly animated and began to share story after story about his growing up experiences. While the old farmhouse built by his father and older brothers was gone, the dairy barn still stood at the bottom of a hill and I took a photo of Dad standing in front it, beaming proudly.

It was when we got back into the Buick and started down the road along the ridge away from the farm that it was time to put the final piece of my plan into action—beginning with my silently engaging the child locks on the back doors. I didn't think Dad would try to escape from the car, but I wasn't going to take any chances. Then I began to ask a series of questions about the farm, about who lived there at what time and when various children had moved out. The questions forced him to reflect—taking him back to events that had occurred a half-century before—but Dad was very forthcoming with his answers, until I got to the point about which I was most curious and most intentional.

"Did Leslie ever live in the Heathen Ridge farmhouse?" I began. I followed with a series of fairly innocuous questions about

Fix Your Family

Leslie: what he had done during the war, when he got married, what he had done afterwards, where he and his family had lived. The more questions I asked about Leslie, the shorter and terser my father's answers, became until he was responding with short phrases and then single words. I wondered if he realized I was driving slower and slower along the road that led away from Heathen Ridge. The tension must have been obvious, since the others in the car with us were sitting in complete silence. I wondered if they were familiar with the information I was seeking from Dad.

"So you were at home when the sheriff showed up and said they found Leslie's car?" I asked. Prior to that moment, my father probably didn't know I'd ever heard of that event.

There was a long moment of silence. Then Dad sort of sighed and he began to describe the evening the sheriff came to the farmhouse. I pulled to the side of the road, listening carefully as he described the scene, his memory of it quite vivid.

When he had finished, I asked, "Did you all ever figure out what happened to him?"

At that point my aunt and her daughter spoke up. Each had heard a different rumor about Leslie and his disappearance—neither of which was remotely like the report my mother had given me about what happened to him.

"No," Dad said, shaking his head and beginning to weep. "Here's what I heard." Then he told a totally different story.

Each of the four possible tales was plausible. We sat there on the side of the road, reflecting on the missing brother/uncle.

"So," I asked, "has there never been a general discussion among the family about Leslie and what happened to him?"

"No," my aunt replied. "I don't think any of us ever talked about this 'out loud' at all."

"Well," I said, as I put the car into gear and started back down the road, "we've got to hurry or we'll be late for supper."

Over the next few minutes, I could feel the anxiety in the car dissipate. A calm conversation about a variety of matters commenced. By the time we got to my uncle's house, my father was more energized and loquacious than I had ever experienced. He went about embracing, kissing and teasing his relatives. Had I been a stranger, I would have guessed that this was a party meant *to celebrate my father's return from a distant trip. I do not remember him ever expressing such joy and excitement.*

The next day, before we went our separate ways, Dad produced a handwritten list of his relatives whom I did not know and began to tell me their stories. I very much had the feeling that it was suddenly okay for him to discuss people and matters that had been previously walled off.

As I was preparing to leave, one of my uncles stopped me and said solemnly, as if this had been a matter long deliberated, "You know, we like you."

That Sunday afternoon in a red Buick Century driving along the road from Heathen Ridge to the state highway, I detonated a love bomb. I had given thought to the stuck place I wanted to unstick (*my father's unwillingness to discuss his family history and in particular the disappearance of my uncle Leslie*), had mapped out a plan complete with time and place (*getting him "at my mercy" in the car after visiting family memorials and his childhood home place*) and determined how I was going to broach the unacceptable, unmentionable, unspeakable subject (*asking a series of questions that proceeded from being innocuous to being totally confrontational*). Apart from knowing I was not going to let Dad out of the car until he addressed those questions, I had no design about what was going to happen after I had finished asking everything I had prepared. I suspect it was extremely awkward for my dad as my pointed questions built toward the very subject and event of which he had never spoken. Maybe that was a terrible thing for me to do. I do know he was like a joyous child afterwards and his new spirit permeated the entire family gathering. I also suspect that, had I not pinned him down about Leslie's disappearance, he would have gone to his grave fourteen years later without ever having spoken aloud about his brother or having given me the list of other relatives he had determined he wanted me to hear about and investigate.

Now, in case you should decide to loosen some stuckness in your family in a meaningful way, we're going to walk through the steps of how to go about planning, planting and detonating a love bomb. We're going to use a different family constellation—the Post/Tucker family—as an illustration of how the process works. We'll set the stage with the first part of the vignette, that portion designed to reveal the unyielding stuckness in the family.

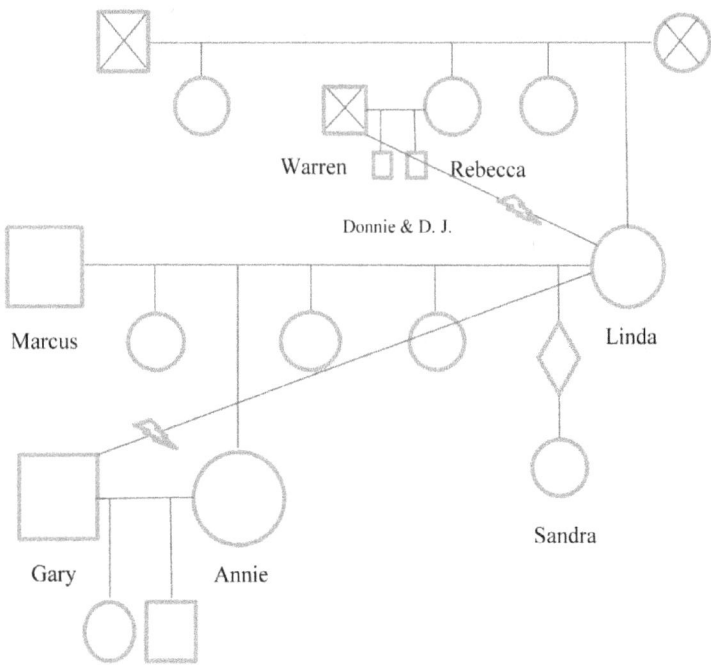

This is the Post/Tucker family. For the sake of simplicity and clarity, the images of other family members and the names of some relatives have been omitted. Note that Linda had a conflicted relationship with Warren, the deceased husband of her second born sister. Linda also has a conflicted relationship with Gary, the husband of her daughter Annie.

When Gary Tucker saw the little stationery-sized letter from his mother-in-law, Linda Post, he assumed she was writing to thank him. After all, he had given her a full set of the photos he had taken a couple weeks before during the family gathering at the Post farm, their personal, little rural retreat from the bustle of city life. And she might have been thanking him as well for all the work he had done around the farmhouse—setting up beds, cleaning up after all the kids, and especially helping Marcus, his father-in-law, who was still recovering from bypass surgery.

Usually when his grandkids came to the farm, Marcus was the

one who took the kids on long hikes through the woods or prepared their fishing tackle and took them fishing at the pond. Over the long July 4th weekend, Gary had been the only one of the Posts' four sons-in-law who came to the farm. Accordingly he decided just to step into the caregiver role and make sure everything worked as it should for the gaggle of grandchildren.

He was eager to be helpful in part because he and his mother-in-law had gone through a lengthy period of shared, thinly veiled hostility. Gary wanted to demonstrate he had no animosity toward Linda, despite her sharp words and the obvious dislike and disapproval she exuded toward him. Perhaps, through his considerate, unassuming behavior, at last the discord between them could be overcome.

At least that was what he thought before he opened the envelope and read the six pages within. She began her letter by castigating him for allowing Marcus to be involved with the grandchildren in any way. Wasn't Gary aware, she asked, of his delicate, dangerous condition? Why hadn't he insisted that his father-in-law remain in the farmhouse. Systematically she criticized everything he had done over the holiday weekend—from playing favorites with his own two children and not lavishing enough attention on the six others who were present, to not stepping in to take over the grilling duties when Marcus decided he wanted to cook hotdogs and hamburgers, to making too much noise outside when Marcus and she were trying to take a nap.

After criticizing his most recent sins, she began to go backward in time through her catalog of his misdeeds, culminating in his marrying her second born daughter. She ended by demanding an apology. Never once did she express appreciation for what he had done for the family or thank him for the photos—even though Gary knew she loved photos of her grandchildren, and sometimes snatched prints without asking his permission.

He couldn't help but notice that her handwriting, which at first was even and easily legible on the unlined stationery, gradually became larger and uneven so that, by the end of the letter, it was as if two different people had written it. Her rage directed at him was so obvious it fairly dripped from the paper. He read the letter through a second time, trying to decide how to respond. He was more amazed than angry, but he knew he had to reply to her in some way. One thing was for certain, his efforts at appeasement and conciliation had been wasted.

Gary went to his scanner and printed out a copy of all six pages Linda had written to him. He sat down at his computer and composed a very calm response. He spelled out the things he had done over the holiday weekend, expressing that he had kept an eye on his father-in-law the whole time and had taken as much of the load as Marcus would allow him; that Marcus had insisted on participating to the extent he was physically able.

Expressing that it had been his intention to mend fences with her by being the consummate caregiver over the weekend, Gary wrote that he was somewhat surprised that she hadn't seemed aware of all he had done without being asked. He was also surprised that she didn't thank him for the great photos of the grandkids he had passed along.

As he continued the letter, he told Linda he had been aware from his first participation in her family, beginning the year before he and Annie had gotten married, that Linda had disliked him and that, despite his best and concerted efforts, over the years her dislike had festered until she truly despised him. The letter was concluded with his proclamation that he had no intention of ever seeing her again and would not be accompanying Annie and their children on any future trips to visit Linda and Marcus.

"Not that they ever would," Gary wrote, "but if your friends should ask you why Annie's husband never comes with her to see you anymore, you just show them the copy of your letter I'm enclosing. Once they read it, they will understand perfectly why I have no intention of ever being around you again."

So that his wife would not be blindsided by the communication between him and her mother, after he mailed the letter, Gary told her what he had written. He also let her read the letter Linda had sent to him.

Annie considered what he had told her for a few moments, then said, "You know she's not going to accept this, right?"

"Why wouldn't she? She's hated me since day one. Now she's rid of me. Isn't that exactly what she's wanted all along?"

Annie, however, turned out to be correct. Within a few weeks, two of her sisters and their families contacted the Tuckers to tell them they would be coming to visit during the fall. Each family lived within a few dozen miles of Marcus and Linda and their trips would be more than 400 miles one way. It was the first time either of her sisters had come to visit. And each of the visits, which were pleasant and light-hearted, was concluded with the sisters and brothers-in-law saying, "Now we'll see all of you this Christmas at Mom's house."

Gary did not correct them or say anything at all. Instead he mused over this strange procession. Clearly these two families had been directed by Linda to travel all the way to the Tucker's house to assert that Annie and Gary were expected to be present as always at the annual Christmas family gathering.

As if that message had not been expressed clearly enough, right before the first of November, Marcus called. He visited for several minutes with Annie and asked about his grandchildren. Before he hung up, he asked to speak to Gary. Their conversation was quite cordial and casual, with Marcus expressing a lot more interest in Gary's life than he ever had before. It was concluded with Marcus saying, "We're looking forward to seeing the Tucker family at Christmas. And, Gary, that means we're expecting to see you too."

A couple days after the phone call, Gary had a little family confab at the end of supper. He told his wife, daughter and son that he knew they had been following this little drama. He pointed out that two family units had made the long trip to see them specifically to make say the whole Tucker family was to be present for the Christmas gathering and that Grandpa Marcus had specifically instructed him to attend.

"You know, I had been anticipating that, rather than driving, you two and your mother could fly to see your grandparents. It would be quicker, even though your mom doesn't like to fly. You certainly would not need me if you traveled that way. Now I'd like to take a vote. How many of you want me to go back with you to Granny and Pa Pa's house for Christmas?"

The three others sitting around the table raised their hands.

"And how many want me to stay right here?"

Gary raised his hand.

He smiled. "Unfortunately, this is not a democracy. I'm going to do what I think is best for me. I will take your desires into consideration. And, anyway, one way or another, we will all have a good Christmas."

The Three Steps

There are three steps or stages involved in planning and carrying out a nodal event, or "love bomb." Each is preceded by a question and each comes with a caution.

Step one is to **discover and focus on the essential stuckness in your family that you want to attack**. The implied question is, *have you investigated your family enough to be reasonably certain that you have found the key stuck point*? The caution is, *no one can fully know the causes, extent or nuances of the stuckness that exists within the family system or the individuals caught up in the dynamic of being stuck*. These ideas, when boiled down to their essence, mean that you can never know everything involved with the stuckness in the family and—if the love bomb works—you are in for some unpredictable results, some revelations that cannot be anticipated.

By way of illustration, consider the stuckness in my dad's family surrounding his missing brother. Having grown up in the family, it wasn't too difficult for me to figure out that Leslie's disappearance was a true sticking point. This didn't mean I knew why it had the impact on the family it did, or that my father would or could explain it.

The resulting unstuckness was not revealed through Dad offering some soliloquy about the mystery of losing his beloved brother and the emotional impact it had on him. You should not expect that from anybody. The unstuckness was revealed in the emotional release he evidenced in his reaction after the conversation on Heathen Ridge and the new freedom to discuss his family that came from it. There was no way I could have anticipated that he would immediately create a list of relatives and task me with learning about them.

The serendipitous presence of my aunt and cousin and their joining in the conversation about what happened to Leslie was a further revelation to me that the whole, big family had been stuck around what happened to Leslie. Thus I was pretty much on target when it came to where the Simpson family was stuck, but I didn't anticipate the magnitude of the stuckness or how the extended members of my family of origin would respond.

Now let's fill in some of the blanks surrounding the

Post/Tucker family so we can get a glimpse of the information Gary will use as he prepares his love bomb:

By the time of the Christmas Showdown described above, Gary had been a part of the Post family's activities and routines for more than two decades, including twenty years of marriage to Annie, the second born daughter of Linda and Marcus. Literally from the moment he met Linda, his future mother-in-law had expressed a distaste for him. During their year of dating before they married, he had asked Annie why her mother had such an obvious dislike for him.

"You're kind of a smart aleck and know-it-all, Gary," Annie said. "Maybe if you back off on that a little bit she won't give you such a hard time."

In the years that followed, Gary vacillated between trying to appease Linda and getting so fed up with her animosity that he freely spoke his mind. There were times when he decided to be absent from the family gatherings; in those days they lived only thirty miles from the Post's home. When Linda got wind that Gary wasn't going to attend one of the holidays or birthday parties—all of which the family celebrated together—she would call Annie and harangue her until Annie begged Gary not to miss the gathering. Gary, totally confused, would comply. It was beyond him to understand why Linda simultaneously hated him yet demanded his presence at family events. Even after he took a job that required him to move his family 400 miles away, Linda still insisted that the Tuckers be present for every possible family celebration.

Over the years Gary had also pieced together an historical picture of Linda's birth family. She had been the youngest of four girls. The second born sister, Rebecca, was ten years older than Linda. Rebecca had married a fellow named Warren Davis. Warren, a serviceman during World War II, was not particularly liked by the other members of Linda's family. He came across as a fellow who thought he knew everything. In particular he had not gotten along with Linda. She was about ten when Warren came into the family and he seemed to go out of his way to tease and provoke her. In his investigations, Gary got the sense that Warren had truly liked Linda and that his teasing her was more to get her attention and interact with her than anything malicious. For her part, Linda just wanted Warren to leave her alone. After Linda had met and married Marcus, there came a point at which Warren took a job in New Jersey and moved his family there, far from where Rebecca and Linda had grown up. This was the first family household to move away from northeastern Ohio and Linda felt particularly angry at Warren. He had, in her estimation, stolen her sister and nephews and disrupted the closeness of the family.

The relationship between Warren and Rebecca had long been contentious and her family was concerned that Warren wasn't respectful toward Rebecca and their boys. There was even some thought that he was abusive. Rebecca packed her sons up after half a dozen years in New Jersey and moved them back to her hometown.

This return preceded the lingering death of Linda and Rebecca's mother by only a couple months. As they gathered in preparation for the funeral, Warren showed up—unannounced and quite inebriated. When the other sons-in-law told him to leave, that he could not attend the funeral, Warren left. After the service, when everyone went back to the family home for a meal, Warren showed up again, standing on the front porch in a stupor, demanding to come in and speak to his estranged wife. Several of the men furiously announced they were going to go out and deal with him. At that point, Linda spoke up.

"You guys are just going to beat him up. Then you'll have that to live with every time you think of today and Mom's funeral. Becca, you need to just stay inside and let me handle Warren."

She went onto the front porch and told Warren that he could not enter, that he could not see Rebecca or his boys and that he had to leave. More words were passed between them, only increasing Linda's ire until at last she spoke a final pronouncement: "Leave, Warren. None of us ever want to see you again."

Warren did indeed depart. About six months later authorities in New Jersey contacted Rebecca to tell her Warren was dead. He had died in a drunk driving accident.

As Gary mused over the story about Linda and Warren, it came to him that there were a number of similarities between himself and the troublesome, deceased brother-in-law. He began to believe that Linda had some unfinished emotional business with Warren and that she was trying in a way to work them out with Gary. The question was, how could he address this with Linda? He knew that simply pointing out the connection would not alleviate Linda's behavior. Fixing this would require some sort of emotional encounter—a love bomb.

This takes us to the second step in the process, **conceiving of an event or series of events that specifically, precisely, intentionally, emotionally shine light on the point of stuckness in a way that is not hostile, judgmental or predictive**. The question that arises here is, *what can you do to focus the family or the right individuals in it upon the emotional content of the stuckness that binds them in a way that is not negative?* The caution—and this one is particularly important—is to remember that *what you are planning and planting is a love bomb and therefore is not to be negative in any way*; you are not seeking revenge; you are not trying to get that hard-headed family member to wake up and see things your way.[xxx]

If this book has made sense to you and, as a result, you've reflected on the real emotional process at work in your family, then the people you love most in the world have become in large measure transparent to you. You grasp their motives and true emotions, very likely, better than they do. This knowledge is not a license to afflict your family members by confronting them with realities they may never be ready to deal with. Rather, with these new learnings you have been imbued with a new responsibility: your task is to help your family in a compassionate way encounter the points of stuckness that are binding them.

Maybe you are not yet willing to help certain family members become unstuck. *If you can't put aside your anger and plan and plant a love bomb from a place of genuine affection for your loved ones, then please go pray and meditate until you can.* I promise your family will stay stuck until you are ready to work with them from a place of accepting love.

Before we go back to the saga of Gary and Linda, I'd like to share a story about a perfect love bomb that was detonated in my home when I was fourteen. Let me preface this by saying one of the more annoying themes of my childhood was that I was constantly being accused of doing bad things that I had not done (which is not to say I hadn't done plenty of ornery things and gotten away with them, but still).

When I was in the eighth grade, I stayed at my grandparents' home after school most days until my dad got off work, picked me up and took me out to our farm. On one occasion I was accused of pocketing money that belonged to my grandparents: they gave me some money to buy a gallon of milk and sent me to the store with my uncle. The way they told it, when I got home, I did not give them the change for that purchase. When I heard this, I insisted that I had turned the change over to them. A huge fight ensued and escalated until both my parents were involved. All this was over less than two dollars. Eventually it became clear that I had not taken the money, but by that time I had informed my parents I was not ever going to Grandma and Grandpa's house again. This transpired late in winter and, being the bullheaded person I was, I persistently refused for the next five or six months to go to my grandparents' home or to be at any place where I might encounter them.

Late in the summer, a couple months after my fourteenth birthday, my grandparents appeared unannounced at our farm one night. They had been to church, by the way they were dressed, and they came into the living room and went to the sofa and just sat there. I took that as my cue to go check on the livestock; who knows what the chickens and hogs might be up to when it's getting dark. I sat out on the fence by the outbuildings for half an hour or so—facing away from the house—and eventually my dad came wandering down.

"You know they're really here to see you, of course."

I did know that. I didn't say a word.

"It took a lot for them to do this. You might think about coming in and speaking to them at least."

With that he turned and went back up the hill. I don't think I recognized at the time how much respect my grandparents were extending to me or how much freedom my parents were granting me. As I say, don't expect the people you "bomb" to grasp the emotional profundity of the moment. However, they might—as I did—make the right decision and walk back up to the house.

I remember coming through the back door and seeing my grandparents still sitting there on the sofa, but frankly I don't remember what was said afterward. I feel a lot of warmth and love when I think about that moment though. And what's really important is, for the rest of their lives there was nothing but love and respect exchanged between us. They detonated a love bomb that night in the living room of our farmhouse. It changed things between us for the better forever.

In a sense, Gary had been preparing to plant and detonate this love bomb for more than twenty years. He knew the family Christmas Day ritual perfectly. He knew the arrangement of the furniture in the Posts' house and where the various members of the family would be as the time approached for everyone to sit down in their "sharp casual" attire for supper.

He knew it would stoke a great deal of anxiety if he interacted with Linda; after all, everyone knew that Gary had been refusing to attend because of the letter Linda sent him. He knew that, if he remained calm and stayed out of the way, the level of anxiety would diminish, but that he could stoke it up again the instant he chose to interact with Linda.

Gary also knew that Linda had unresolved issues with her deceased brother-in-law, Warren. It must have troubled her, Gary guessed, that she had assumed the responsibility of dealing with Warren and sent him away with the assertion no one ever wanted to see him again, only to have him die shortly afterwards with no resolution of the hostility between them.[xxxi] *He knew the unfinished business between Warren and Linda was symbolically living on in the relationship between Linda and himself. This helped him understand the total illogic of Linda's detesting him yet emotionally refusing to let go of him.*

Gary came to believe that if he—and probably he was the only one who could do it—could ask Linda the right questions about Warren in the right way, something would break loose; indeed, something would break loose between Linda and Gary as well as between Linda and her memories of Warren.

Now that Gary has his fully developed plan in mind, let's see how he detonates this love bomb. This takes us to the third step or stage in implementing a nodal event in our families: **strive to remain connected and non-anxious as you follow completely through with your plan**. The implied question is, *will you actually be able to follow through with the plan you have devised*? And accordingly, the caution is, *once you get started on detonating the love bomb, don't chicken out part way through and above all, do not stop in the middle and try to explain what you're doing.*[xxxii] If you get halfway through a series of events or questions and then give in to your anxiety and try to drop the whole thing, the emotional responses you will receive will range from extreme confusion to outrage. Once you start, see it through. Yes, there will be some "heart-in-throat" moments at the peak of the experience. Those are an indication you are in close proximity to the emotional state you are trying to address.

Also, an extra little caution here: *just because people have an adverse reaction to the love bomb, do not assume you have failed.* Only on television melodramas does a family member step up, suddenly enlightened, and say, "Thank you for showing me the narrowness of my vision and helping me see these past events in a new light." In my experience, a love bomb has worked when those who experience it become reflective, perhaps show some emotion and afterwards express a lightness characterized by heightened excitement, energy and joy. And while we're at it, a successful love bomb frequently unleashes a cascade of responses, most of which indicate a new empowerment at work within the family. We will talk more about that below and also in the chapter on the history of Bowen Theory/Emotional Process.

Before we get to how Gary bombed his mother-in-law (sorry, couldn't resist), I want to give one more example of a love bomb that worked—this one from a fictitious source: *The Rifleman.* You have to be older than dirt to remember this TV western from the early 60s in which a farmer named Lucas McCain found some reason every week to use his rifle like a six-shooter and blast away a few bad guys. Lucas was best friends with a sheriff, an older fellow named Micah.

In one episode Micah became obsessed with the fear that he was no longer up to doing the job of protecting the little town of Northfork.[xxxiii] In particular Micah was troubled because a gunslinger—a man he had sent to prison who wore thick eyeglasses and vowed he would get revenge on Micah—had gotten out of the penitentiary. For most of the episode, Micah sat around in a drunken haze, scared that he could not stop this bad guy who was coming to gun him down. Finally, terrified, he went to another town to hide out. Lucas, of course, found him and tried to persuade him he was up to the task of handling this outlaw—but to no avail (remember: the "carefully reasoned response" never works). Sitting in a saloon, drinking himself to oblivion, Micah was startled to see the gunfighter enter and sit down beside him at the table. The outlaw couldn't help but gloat as he told Micah how long he'd been waiting for his revenge.

"How did you find me?" Micah asked.

"That's the best part," the villain said. "Your friend Lucas McCain told me where you were."

There was a momentary struggle with the concept of what had happened, then the light of revelation spread across his face. Micah said, "I can't believe he did that for me."

In the next instant he snatched off the bad guy's spectacles and, when the outlaw reached for them instead of his pistol, Micah smacked him over the head with a whiskey bottle. I guess the guy went back to prison after that. In those days most TV westerns were only half an hour long, so it's hard to know exactly what happened to him. Farfetched as that is, the emotions portrayed are real. They resonate with us.

So, staying with the illustration, can you imagine what a risk Lucas was taking when he told the bad guy where to find his friend? Chances are, you aren't going to put any of your family members at the risk of dealing with a murderous outlaw, but it's very likely there will be a heart-pounding moment as you follow through with your plans.

Gary waited until the week of Thanksgiving before he announced to his family at supper one night that he had reached a decision. "I don't really want to go with you this Christmas. It's nothing against any of you of course. Still, I've been giving this a lot of thought. Your mother hates to fly and her 'safe person'—me—will not be there to fly with her. Flying will double the expense of the trip and therefore cut back on the gifts your mom and I want to get you for Christmas. So I've decided to drive you all to Granny and Pa Pa's for Christmas."

"And you're going to be with us the whole time, right?" his daughter asked.

"If I'm welcome in the house, I guess I will."

"You know you are welcome in my parents' house," Annie retorted. "We are all glad you are going, dear. And to make this a happy holiday, you need to be on your best behavior."

"Are you going to tell your mother the same thing?" he asked without looking at her.

Gary suspected that the news of his decision would quickly permeate through the gossip chain and that the entire Post clan would settled back to its normal state of emotional balance. Everyone would assume, he knew, that Linda and he would mostly dodge each other during the family's time of gathering and all would therefore be "okay." For his part, Gary mentally rehearsed and refined what he was going to ask Linda and when he would ask it.

Linda and Marcus greeted the Tuckers at the front door, hugging the grandchildren and Annie. Marcus gave Gary a hearty handshake and Linda gave him curt "Hello" beneath Annie's watchful gaze. Gary proceeded to fade into the background of the fellowship as different households of the Post clan arrived. Christmas Eve came and went with no dialogue at all between Linda and himself. He could feel people beginning to relax and just enjoy the reunion.

Christmas day was a relaxed time of grandchildren playing with their new gifts, the adults playing card games and sons-in-law making numerous trips out to the backyard to enjoy cigars in the unusually pleasant weather. Gary participated, mostly focusing on remaining in the background.

When 4:30 p.m. came around, he sat down in the Martha Washington chair facing the clock on the wall just outside the hallway leading to the master bedroom. He held a thick, hardback book in his hand and read slowly. From the corner of his eye he could see all the activity taking place in the kitchen. This year, as with every year in his memory, Linda was directing her four daughters as they prepared the Christmas feast, which was to begin promptly at 5:30. Just before 5 p.m., he knew, Linda would give final instructions to her girls and scurry to her bedroom to get dressed and fix her hair and makeup before everyone sat down to eat.

Sure enough, right at 4:50, Linda said something to one of Annie's sisters about putting rolls in the oven and started toward her bedroom. Just as she was passing by Gary, he lowered the book and said with a curious expression, "Linda, I have a question for you."

Instantly everyone in the kitchen and den where Gary sat ceased talking and moving. Linda, who was startled by this sudden address, stopped and looked toward him.

"Was your sister Rebecca the only blonde in the family?" he asked.

The question—totally unexpected and disconnected from anything going on at that moment—took her completely off guard. "Um, yes. Well, you know, she was a bleached blonde."

"Oh, like Annie. And her husband was Warren, right?"

"Yes. He was her first husband."

"And didn't they have a couple kids?"

"Uh, Donnie and D.J."

"So, he was in the service when they got married?"

"Well, he was in the Army just before war started and I guess he had known Becca before that. Maybe they had dated in high school. But when he came home on furlough before going overseas, they decided to get married."

Gary nodded. "I think a lot guys did that."

"My sister Minnie did the same thing. Her husband Leroy was a sailor."

"But then, when the war was over, he came back and they lived in your hometown?"

The conversation continued with Gary asking a number of simple, historical questions—to most of which he already knew the answers. At a certain point, he mentioned that he had heard that Warren was sort of an annoying fellow. As the dialogue continued, Linda's answers grew longer and more detailed. She first leaned against the other Martha Washington chair that faced Gary, then sat down on the edge of it facing him. Linda gave an accounting of how Warren had pestered and provoked her.

"He used to say I was spoiled because I was the baby. Well Daddy was a plumber and Momma stayed home and we didn't have anything. None of us were spoiled."

"Why was he such a jerk to you?"

Tears began to form in the corners of her eyes as Linda answered. "I think he just didn't know how to be around people. He was an only child and he just didn't understand."

Gary nodded. "And I guess it just got worse."

"Oh, yes." She sat back in the chair. "When Becca moved off with him to New Jersey, I thought I would be glad to be rid of him, but I couldn't stop thinking about my sister being stuck with that guy."

"Well she moved home, didn't she?"

"Oh, just before Momma died. And then he showed up drunk after Momma's funeral." Her words tailed off.

After a moment of silence, Gary said quietly, "I guess he never got it. I am sorry he missed out, that he never got a handle on how much love there can be in big family like this." He glanced up at the clock above her head. "Oh my goodness! Have I made you late?"

Linda looked at the clock as well and hopped to her feet. "I've got to change." She disappeared into the bedroom.

As Gary got up, he was aware that people around him were beginning to speak quietly and to move around again. The members of the family had been listening to the conversation. He stretched and walked out to the front yard, where a half dozen grandsons were playing football. As he stood on the porch, he heard determined footsteps approaching him—a sound he identified as belonging to Annie.

She came outside and stood beside him. "I heard you talking to my mother."

"Well," he said, "you heard me speaking to her about a smart aleck who married the second born bleached blonde daughter, relocated the family hundreds of miles away from everyone else and never got along with Linda. Was I talking about me, or was I talking about Warren?"

Linda considered the question. "Okay. I just don't want there to be any more friction between you two."

He nodded. "Nope. I think it's going to be okay."

Several minutes later everyone gathered inside, the children at the two small tables and the grownups around the elongated dining table. It was exactly 5:30. From where he stood silently, Gary saw Linda sigh and grasp Marcus' hand.

"We're so glad that everyone is here and healthy," she pronounced. "This year for the blessing I'd like to ask Gary to say the prayer."

Two days later, as the Tucker family departed, Linda gave Gary a fierce hug and kiss on the cheek. "Thanks for coming."

"I was very glad to be here."

Dr. Mike Simpson

Now What?

In a way, detonating a love bomb can seem terribly anticlimactic. I don't think this dynamic—a real, intentionally conducted event that breaks down the stuckness in a family—will ever attract much attention in the movies or on TV because it almost seems that nothing has happened. At the time Linda got up from the Martha Washington chair to change clothes, or my dad got out of the back seat of the Buick Century or the lady who asked Murray Bowen for some sleeping pills to kill herself actually showed up the next morning, it seemed as if no life-changing dramatic event has transpired. Emotional shockwaves don't necessarily register on the Richter Scale. But that doesn't mean they aren't very real. And they are often life-changing.

So what should you expect? What does happen after a successful love bomb is detonated in your family?

First, *you may recognize a sense of relief, release, energy, excitement and joy pervading those who experience the love bomb.* You may have heard the expression that there is a spirit beyond our understanding which sometimes overwhelms the sorrow, injustice, pain and one's intellectual grasp of life; and you might recognize the presence of such a spirit after the love bomb goes off. It's difficult to describe the sensation and its tangible symptoms without resorting to metaphors, but I suppose you could say this experience is like people who have had their memories wiped clean are suddenly able once again to remember those things that brought them joy and those people whom they loved. It doesn't take long before they react to that sensation accordingly.

Second, *over the long term you may see lasting positive change in those impacted by the love bomb.* As I indicated in the story about my father, he wasn't just energized after I lured him into talking about his brother. Afterwards he demonstrated a willingness to discuss and investigate his family's history. Just as the relationship I had with my grandparents remained positive and constant for the rest of their lives, I'm told there was never bitterness again between Linda and Gary (at this writing, the Christmas Standoff is two decades in the past). This is not to say that other stuck places don't exist in families who have experienced a positive nodal event (as you will see with #4 below). This is merely an observation that once a stuck point is successfully dislodged, stuckness around that issue doesn't seem to reoccur.

Third, *new ideas and new creativity seem to burst forth in the aftermath of a nodal event.* It's almost as if the emotional stuckness in a family system also diminishes the intellectual possibilities of those who are stuck within the system.[xxxiv] Once the stuckness is overcome, those positive things that have been bottled up just burst forth.

The example of this that comes to my mind most clearly has to do with the death of Ed Friedman. We "Ed-Heads" were devastated by his sudden death and all of us felt tremendous loss and a sense of directionlessness. Yet one year later when we gathered on Columbus Day, 1997, to celebrate his life it was astonishing to hear about the stunning variety of ways in which different students and protégés of Ed had taken his work and principles and applied them in unique ways. For my part, within the eleven months following his death, I had created the Lazarus Project and was already at work using Bowen Theory to help revitalize declining congregations. You and others in your family may likewise discover new directions and the power to pursue them in the wake of a love bomb.

Fourth, *with successful nodal events there is almost always a* **cascade effect**, *that is, an ongoing series of freeing, empowering aftershocks that are indirect results of the love bomb.* Probably the most famous record of this can be read in Ed Friedman's essay, "The Birthday Party Revisited," to which I alluded previously. This essay, along with many of Ed's other Family Systems writings, is worth tracking down and reading (you'll find a list of suggested additional readings at the end of the text, after the addenda, just prior to the endnotes, near the back cover but before the ISBN number; or you can just check the table of contents for the page number). Anyway, as his mother's 70th birthday approached, Ed wanted to overcome some points of stuckness in his family and in particular to work on some emotional distance he perceived between himself and his mom. He landed on the idea of a surprise birthday party in large measure because Ed was generally considered the least likely person in his family to do such a thing. Not only was this love bomb an astonishing success, but members of his extended family continued to report changes, new insights and new growth—that they attributed to this single event—not just for years, but for decades following the actual party. And by the way, Ed and his mom got pretty close after that.

I'd like to give another example of the cascade effect. After that I promise I'll quit talking about Gary and Linda.

Several weeks after the Christmas Standoff, Linda contacted Annie to ask her if she remembered her foster sister Sandra. Over a period of several decades Linda and Marcus had been foster parents for dozens of children. By far the child the Posts had fostered the longest and loved the most was Sandra. She was bi-racial infant given up by her mother at the time of her birth. Sandra came to live with the Posts when she only a few days old and remained with them until she was almost five. Just prior to her fifth birthday, a female relative of Sandra's who had children about the same age found out that this child existed and asked to bring her into her home. Just like that, Sandra was gone. To three of the Post girls, however, this was like losing a sister who had grown up with them (sister number four didn't come along for another year).

Annie was excited to learn that Linda had gone to the trouble of tracking down Sandra, who was now a single career woman living in Florida. For her part, Sandra was delighted to hear from her foster mother. She had never forgotten Linda, Marcus and the girls. Indeed she said she always felt as if they were her real family.

Over the course of nearly a year, the correspondence continued and expanded. They learned about Sandra's childhood after she left them. The Posts brought Sandra up to speed on what had happened in their house. Then, as the holidays approached, Marcus and Linda asked if Sandra would accept a round-trip airline ticket as a Christmas present, so that they could officially be reunited.

When Sandra's flight was about to land on Christmas day, Gary found himself sitting in the notorious Martha Washington chair in the Post's family room reading a newspaper. He was somewhat surprised to hear Linda—who had orchestrated the arrival of her foster child—ask Marcus and their youngest daughter, who had never met Sandra, if they would go to the airport to pick her up. Once they had departed, Linda called her other three daughters into the kitchen. Gary waited for her to ask him to leave, but Linda seemed content with him sitting where he could overhear the conversation.

Tears beginning to fall, she said, "There's something I have to tell you. When the county contacted me to tell me that Sandra's relatives found out about her and wanted her to live with them, they gave me a choice. They said Sandra could stay with us if we would adopt her." Linda's hands and face began to quiver. "I thought about this for a long time—as much time as they would give us to make the decision. Finally I decided to let her go. I thought it would be better for her if she were raised by a black family who were her real relatives. The minute she was gone, I knew I had made a mistake."

The sisters all began to cry, hugging their mother. They stood together in the kitchen embracing one another. One after another, they thanked Linda for sharing this with them and told her they understood how she must have felt and what a tough position she had been in.

As their conversation ended, Gary rose and went into the kitchen, ostensibly to get a cup of coffee. He stood beside Linda, who was compiling the ingredients of a recipe.

"That must have been incredibly difficult for you," he said. "I guess regret comes with the territory of being a parent. God knows I've made more than my share of mistakes just by trying to be a good dad."

Linda nodded, wiping her nose with a tissue she stuffed back into an apron pocket.

Gary continued, "Seems like sometimes we use our very best judgment in deciding what's right for our children and afterwards we find out there were things we didn't know, or things we misjudged. The problem is, we can't undo it. And we can't explain it, because children can't understand the reasons for the decisions we make, any more than they can understand why they need to be vaccinated." He blew across the top of his coffee cup. "But you know what? In a few minutes you'll be holding that child in your arms and I'll bet none of that regret will even matter."

Linda turned to him and hugged him, clinging to him for a moment. Then she let go wordlessly and went back to cooking.

As he walked out to the backyard, gazing at the snowy

Dr. Mike Simpson

Christmas provided by Mother Nature, he had a pretty good idea that this reunion was an indirect offshoot of their conversation from the previous Christmas. Linda had been reviewing her life from a new, powerful place. It occurred to him that Linda had two major sticking points in her past and that he, of all people, had helped her confront both.

Fifth, in the face of this euphoric optimism and empowerment, there has to be a negative, right? *Another strange result of a successful nodal event is physical illness.* If you read the section in the history chapter, Chapter Six, about the Christmas of the Special Child, you'll hear how bizarre physical problems developed among some of us who participated in detonating that amazing love bomb.

And while love bombs often do seem to result in odd symptoms, these physical responses aren't always the result of a love bomb. Simply beginning to use the abilities and strategies described in *Fix Your Family* can sometimes (though certainly not always) result in physical issues.[xxxv] And often people and families get unstuck without having to resort to planning and conducting a nodal event (more about that below).

Ed Friedman once spoke about a faithful student of his who unaccountably missed several workshops. The student contacted Ed to say that he had been sick with a strange brain disorder, but was recovering and would be back to participate in future sessions. The student said it came to him like a revelation that he had made so many changes in his life—upset the balance of his existence to such a degree—that he had physically sabotaged himself. In his birthday party essay, Friedman also describes several family members who had unexpected physical reactions to that nodal event.

One woman who was a member of a church I pastored came to see me several times over the course of a couple months. During one of the last sessions, she confided in me that her daughter had been the victim of a sexual assault perpetrated during a church sponsored event. I noted that, as she related this to me, she didn't seem particularly upset about it. A few days later she appeared again at my office door unannounced, came in and sat down.

"I have something to tell you," she said. "I was driving down the street yesterday and all of the sudden something went wrong with my car. It started surging and getting slower and slower, as if the brakes had locked up or I had several flat tires all at once. I steered over to the curb and as I did, I realized there was nothing wrong with the car, that I was the one who was shaking. I had a death grip on the steering wheel and I was jamming the brake pedal to the floor again and again. Then I heard myself say, 'He raped her! He raped her!'" She took a breath and looked at me. "I had no idea how angry I was until it came out in my body."

The bottom line, I suppose, is that unleashing stuck emotions is going to have an intellectual, physical and—as we've hinted several times—spiritual impact on those who experience it. Fortunately I can report that I've never heard of anyone dying as a result of becoming unstuck. At least not directly.

Do I Have to Bomb Everyone?

Perhaps, if you've waded through all this information and strategy about how to bring about major change through unsticking your family, you're thinking to yourself, "This is way more than I need. I don't want to blast my family into a new place of empowerment. I just want my husband to wake up and carry his share of the family responsibilities. Is it really necessary to go through all these steps and launch a love bomb?"

The short answer to that question is "no." In fact, as you come to understand the emotional processes behind the actions of your loved ones and as you become a well-defined person who is connected to everyone in your family, you are very likely already creating change. The simple reality of knowing where you end and requiring others to recognize and respect those limits without breaking connection with them will often readjust the emotional balance in the family. I think that very dynamic was behind a lot of the changes that we saw happening in the lives of leaders who participated in our Lazarus Project: they grew in confidence and peace of mind and the people with whom they interacted every day found themselves changing as well. As a pastor who worked with conflicted (stuck) families for decades, I often recognized that coaching the leader in a family to become better defined and to stand up for himself/herself would create change and empowerment within other family members as well.

Here is a caution about that, however. If you are trying to

achieve lasting change in a particular relationship and by acting upon the learnings you've acquired from this book you do begin to see the differences you were seeking, *make sure you don't fall back to your old behaviors.* If you want the change you are seeking to be lasting, you must consistently refuse to settle for the old emotional balance.

You may recall the example of Marlene and Griff from the previous chapter. Marlene was the woman who became flustered when her very articulate husband Griff criticized the way she spoke. We coached her on how to deal with Griff in such a way that she did not succumb to his tactic of distraction and she reported the results to be instantaneously positive. Over the course of a few weeks, however, she would let herself fall back into old patterns of appeasing Griff and begging him to comply, requests he found easy to ignore. Then she would contact me again and ask for a "refresher course" in how to get her husband to behave. Permanent change requires that you, as the change agent, permanently refuse to accept the stuckness you have found intolerable.

Let's say, however, that try as you might you can't get the few simple changes in your family that you need, even though you've emerged from studying these ideas with a new sense of who you are and a willingness to attack the stuckness you perceive in your family. Instead of a full-fledge love bomb, maybe just "a baby bomb"—a "love grenade"—will do.

Vanessa deeply loved her husband Glenn, even though she thought once he got home from work in the evening he might be the most useless man alive. He gravitated to the kitchen—where he always found supper ready, even though Vanessa also had a fulltime job—and afterwards lumbered into the den where he plopped onto the couch with the remote and watched television until bedtime. Of course this was only during weekdays. On the weekends he like to bowl and play softball with some of his beer drinking friends, often wandering home magically just in time for supper, and afterwards lying on the couch with the remote.

Fed up with his lethargic behavior and in need of help with caring for the house and their three half-grown children, Vanessa sought advice from her pastor. Over a period of time, she worked on self-definition and acquired a good understanding of the emotion realities behind her slavish willingness to care for her loved ones and for Glenn's apathetic attitude (turns out he was totally babied by his mother and came to view the correct role of a woman as being the absolute servant of the men in her life). Armed with these new awarenesses, Vanessa began to insist that Glenn assist with certain specific chores around the house and with the children. He did respond to her requests, but only reluctantly. Clearly he assumed this was a phase she was going through and, until she got over it, he was going to placate her. He took to rolling his eyes every time she asked for his help and often would ask, "Now what else do you want today, dear? How long is this going to take?"

Vanessa had no desire to continue dealing with his patronizing attitude and lack of willingness to be her partner. She confessed to the minister that she could see only two alternatives. She could either leave him—an idea that overwhelmed her and filled her with grief and dread—or she could just surrender and let things go back to the way they had been for "King Glenn." The pastor suggested a third alternative. Perhaps she could try a sort of mini-nodal event. He coached her as she developed a plan that would dramatically confront her husband with the reality of his behavior and her needs. As the day approached to detonate this "love grenade," Vanessa was asked if she would call the pastor afterward and let him know how things had transpired.

On Wednesday of the following week, Vanessa called the church and asked for the minister. She sounded so disheartened that he feared the whole effort had failed miserably.

"How did go?" he asked.

"Awful."

"Oh. I'm sorry to hear that. So it didn't work?"

"No. It worked perfectly, just like I planned."

"Well . . . then what's so awful?"

She sighed. "I just feel so sorry for poor Glenn."

Vanessa went on to explain that, as she had planned, she came home unexpectedly late from work on Monday. The children were confused and hungry and were raiding the kitchen for snacks. Glenn was lying on the sofa watching TV and peevishly asked her why she was late and where was supper. Calmly she asked him if he had completed the three tasks she had asked him, on Sunday, to do when he got home on Monday.

Dr. Mike Simpson

"Well, no. I—"

She cut him off with a pre-planned explosion of anger. "What is wrong with you! You let your children starve and graze for food because you're too lazy to get off the couch? You don't do anything I ask you to do, but you expect me to have supper on the table for you without being asked? Get out! Get out!"

Stunned and frightened—since he had never seen Vanessa act this way—Glenn scrambled to his feet. "Well, what am I supposed to do?"

"Get out! Get out of here! There is no room in this house for bums. Just get out!"

"Where am I supposed to go?"

This was the question Vanessa had been waiting for. "Your mother's. Go see your mother. She does a lot better job of taking care of you than I do. Now go!"

Thus, without gathering clothes or toothbrush, Glenn grabbed his billfold and keys and stumbled out to his truck. The children, eyes wide, watched their father drive away.

"Mom, where's Dad going?"

She drew a breath to calm herself. "To school."

Late the next morning Glenn called her at her office and asked if she were okay. She informed him that she was fine, but that he had a problem. As the conversation progressed she learned that he had not gone to his mother's house, but spent the night with a friend—who told him it was a "one shot deal."

"I really need to come home."

She continued typing, the phone pressed to her ear. "I'll think about it. Call me back after 4." And she hung up.

When Glenn called back at 4 p.m., Vanessa said, "All right. Here's what I need you to do. I've told the kids to order pizza. Go home and take a shower and put on some nicer clothes. Then meet me at the Mandarin Restaurant at 5 and you can buy my supper. We'll talk over the terms of your coming home."

Vanessa was almost mournful as she related the story to the pastor. She had never seen Glenn so compliant. It was almost pitiful. He had agreed completely to the simple changes Vanessa was demanding (and the Chinese food had been wonderful). And now she felt remorseful. She felt she had tricked her husband and treated him unfairly.

"I can understand your feeling that way. It's an emotional response," the minister said. "Of course intellectually you know that he's been using you as a maid for the past fifteen years and all you're demanding is to be treated like a spouse instead."

"I know you're right," she said. "But still . . ."

"Well you have an interesting decision to make, Vanessa. You can retreat from what you've accomplished and go back to the sort of servitude you were living, or you can act as if you honestly do want things to change for the better permanently. Frankly I think, after the lesson you taught him, you're more likely to knuckle under and go back to the way things were than Glenn is."

Curiosity in her voice, she asked, "Pastor, why are you on my side in this?"

"Nope," he said, "I'm not on your side. When I help you confront Glenn's childish behavior, I'm really ministering to him as well. And I think he probably got this lesson better than anything I ever said in a sermon."

Key ideas set forth in Chapter Five:

- There are three steps or stages involved in planning and carrying out a "love bomb." These include discovering and focusing on the essential stuckness in your family; conceiving of an event or series of events designed to shine light on the point of stuckness; and remaining connected and non-anxious as the events are conducted.
- The most tangible effects of a successful love bomb are a sense of relief, release, energy, excitement and joy pervading those who have experienced the event.
- There are frequently long-term positive results that may take months or years to become evident.
- It is often possible to utilize the principles of Family Systems successfully to confront stuckness and bring about change without a full-fledged love bomb being planned and carried off.

And now, you're ready to confront the stuckness in your family. In the concluding chapter I'll give a brief, amateur history of Bowen Theory with a personal description of what it's meant to me and the ways it has played out in my life.

Dr. Mike Simpson

6
A Brief, Personal History

In July, 1991, a day or two before I left Tulsa to fly to San Francisco and begin work on my doctorate, I called up the board chairman of the congregation I pastored. I wanted to give him a "heads up" about the TLG. The TLG was a small, perpetually disgruntled group of families who had been among the founding members of the five-year-old congregation. TLG ("that little group") was the acronym many other congregants used to refer to them. They were emotionally fused and perpetually on the lookout for a reason to be offended. Any slight or insult—intentional or accidental, actual or perceived—against one of them was taken as an affront by all of them. The saying was, "If we really wanted to get rid of the TLG, you could get them all with one grenade any Saturday night."

"I wanted to warn you about the TLG," I said to the board chair. "It's been almost six weeks since their last eruption, so they are due. I won't be back from California for a month, so you're kind of on your own when it comes to dealing with them."

"I don't think there will be a problem," the chair responded. "After all, you're the one they expect to fix everything they don't like. If you aren't here, they will just sit on their grievances until you get back."

By that time I had already been in the pastoral ministry for eighteen years. I had observed several occasions when a minister left town for vacation or a study trip of some kind while there was controversy brewing, only to discover he had no job to come back to. Because I had an intense desire to keep my finger on the pulse of the congregation, I got up in the pulpit on the last Sunday before my trip and announced that I suffered terribly from homesickness. I asked the membership to send me postcards and letters so I would know that they hadn't forgotten me. I must say, that worked better than I could have imagined. I would guess there were a 120 or so students matriculating at San Francisco Theological

Seminary (SFTS) during the four weeks I was there in late summer, and I easily received more mail than all the other students put together. There was only one family from whom I received no postcards or letters. Sure enough, that was the family that spearheaded the attempt to get rid of me when I got back from California.

I had decided to work on a Doctor of Ministry (DMin) degree as a way of studying spiritual development and SFTS had a wonderful reputation in that area. At our first communal gathering at the seminary, a wine-and-cheese social, I learned that I was supposed to have read all four preliminary textbooks prior to the start of class. This was contrary to what I had been told—that it wasn't necessary to have read the books before we started our matriculation. Well, maybe it wasn't so bad, I thought. After all, I had read three of the four texts. Then the other shoe fell: the first book we were going to discuss was the one book I had not read, *Generation to Generation*, by Dr. Edwin H. Friedman.

The Friedman book had seemed decidedly uninteresting to me: the title was uninspiring, as was the slate gray cover; it was as thick as all the other books put together; and the price had been $25—which was exorbitant in those days. Well, I decided, I need to read the introduction and scan the chapters so at least I could fake knowing something about it. After the social, I retreated to my little bedroom and began to read.

I was not far into the text before I realized it was a work of major insight. Perhaps fifty or seventy-five pages in, it was as if the heavens had opened and brilliant light was shining down upon me. On and on, late into the night, I read. Now I had just flown from Oklahoma to California and my internal clock was set two hours ahead of the actual time; it was very late and I was very tired. Still I read on. It took a supreme act of self-control for me to set the book aside and go to sleep.

Over my years of pastoral ministry, I had acquired an understanding of how people responded in certain ways—an understanding that was never conveyed to me in seminary. In *Generation to Generation*, Ed Friedman revealed to me a coherent framework into which my observations fit, described the emotional reasons behind the actions I had observed and explained to me how to predict and respond to these emotional realities. Over the afternoons and nights that followed, as I continued to study his book—reading and re-reading it—I found that I had a new, clear grasp on why my parishioners—and in particular the TLG—acted as they did. I developed a plan for ministering to that little group. I couldn't wait to get back to Tulsa to unleash my new understanding with action.

But I'm getting ahead of myself.

As I understand it, Murray Bowen was a medical doctor, an Army surgeon during World War II. Though he was offered a position with the Mayo Clinic as a surgeon after the war, Bowen felt himself drawn to psychiatry and in 1946 he started training at the famous Menninger Clinic in Topeka, Kansas. As is the case with psychiatrists in training, he was assigned to one of those groups of patients typically considered "incurable": schizophrenics.

It wasn't long before Bowen noticed an intriguing phenomenon. Whenever one of his schizophrenic clients would start to improve, the family of the patient would begin to act crazy. In his efforts to understand what was going on, Bowen got a grant from the National Institute of Mental Health (NIMH) in Bethesda, Maryland, that allowed him to hospitalize entire families in which there was a schizophrenic individual. His goal from the beginning was not *prescriptive* (to treat people according to a set framework of how mental processes work, like Freudian or Jungian ideology) but rather *descriptive* (to observe how families interacted in a therapeutic setting and from those observations develop an effective treatment method). As he stated clearly in his famous series of essays about this experimental time, *Family Therapy in Clinical Practice*, if a treatment principle they developed worked and accurately depicted what was going on in the family, the principle was retained; if it didn't work, it was discarded. The result of his investigations was a highly effective theory of how human beings group themselves into families and how to work with those families to bring about needed change. This theory is now called Emotional Process, Family Systems, Family Process or Bowen Theory (for some reason, Bowen didn't like the term "Bowen Theory"). The ideas we've lifted up in this book are based on Bowen's insights and theories.

In 1959, Bowen moved his practice from NIMH to

Georgetown University, where he remained and continued refining his insights until his death in 1990. Over the years he accepted a number of students and one of those students was a rabbi named Edwin H. Friedman.

As a clergyman, Friedman had been "through the wars." He had been fired by his congregation during his first pastorate, resulting in a number of the congregants—who felt Friedman had been treated unfairly—breaking away from that synagogue, forming another and calling Ed to be their rabbi.

During his tenure with the new synagogue, Friedman studied with Murray Bowen. While Bowen had intended his theories to be a way of working with sick families, Friedman also recognized the potential for the principles of Emotional Process to be used as a model for effective leadership. One key aspect of this is the view that people invariably form themselves into family groups; when one emerges as a leader within the "family," the group itself becomes open to the leadership of the connected, non-anxious, well-defined individual. Ed was able to put his leadership theory into practice when the same sort of problems that developed during his first pastorate began to surface again in his new congregation. Through the adroit use of Bowen Theory principles, he was able to disarm his critics, to reassert his worthiness to lead and to empower new leaders to emerge within the synagogue.

The recognition of Emotional Process as a powerful leadership tool brought about a sort of evangelistic zeal within Friedman. He wanted to share this discovery with disempowered clergy wherever possible. As a result of that *Generation to Generation* was published in 1985. The book was greeted with great acclaim by clergy around the world and quickly there were multiple printings. Beyond clergy, Friedman extended his leadership principles to business leaders, military leaders, teachers and many other professions. Over the eleven years following the publication of the book, interest in these highly functional leadership ideas grew exponentially. Recognized as a pioneer, Ed was a sought after speaker and consultant for many different organizations, so much so that at the time of his death he had two years of speaking engagements on his calendar.

And that brings me back to where I started this chapter.

Dr. Mike Simpson

In August, 1991, I returned to Tulsa feeling excitement—rather than dread—about facing that little group of hostile parishioners. I set about interacting with them as a group and found different ones of them to be standoffish. I sensed the TLG was up to something. So I sat back patiently to await future developments. Sure enough, there ensued a rather clumsy, two-dimensional attempt to force me out as the pastor. In the natural scheme of things, I suppose I would have alternated between the desire to appease and a desire to attack. Instead of falling back to either of those options—and in an oddly calm and playful mood—I interacted with the leaders of the church to disarm the group.

As a part of my doctoral course work, I wrote a lengthy essay about the TLG and how their attempt to get rid of me—and probably split the church in the process—backfired. While the membership of the church continued to grow rapidly, seven of the eight TLG families left the church within six months. Apparently they weren't much missed.

About a year after that, I accepted a call to a church in Greensboro, North Carolina. It was there I finished my dissertation and received my DMin degree. Within a few weeks of the time my degree was conferred, I asked the congregation for permission to attend Ed Friedman's Post-Graduate Seminar in Family Systems: three sessions over the course of nine months in Bethesda, Maryland. I had met Friedman in person twice before the first workshop, in October, 1995. I also knew that he knew and appreciated the work I had done around dealing with conflict as a pastoral leader. [xxxvi]

As I recall, the sessions ran Tuesday-Wednesday-Thursday. Leaving Monday and Friday as travel days. On the first day before the meeting began, I approached Ed to ask him some question I had about the sessions.

He looked at me closely and said, "You're Mike Simpson."

"Yes, sir. I am."

That was as intimate a communication as I ever had with Ed Friedman. After that I perceived him to be somewhat aloof. I was naturally full of questions and observations, but I kept them pretty much to myself—until I couldn't stand it and I had to ask. Perhaps, I thought, it was just the way he was with everyone, but with me he seemed particularly distant.

At one point Ed briefly discussed his relationship with Murry Bowen, saying that the doctor had confessed to him that he had been an alcoholic. "I think he said things like that," he said, "to keep me from admiring him too much. He wanted me to develop on my own and not be an imitation of him."

What an understatement it would be to say I found that session to be inspiring, enlightening and empowering. I drove south toward North Carolina on I-95, then I-85. In Virginia there are many places where the trees tower above the highways and the road is hilly and curved. It's easy to feel alone and, as the saying goes, "a fellow can do a powerful lot of thinking" on a trip like that. What I was thinking about more than anything was an idea that had come to me during one of the sessions: if it only takes one person to heal a family, and if congregations are family, then it only takes one person to renew a congregation.

I brooded over that for four months until the next session, which fell in mid-February. I remember going up to Friedman before the first session started and asking him if my logical progression was correct. While I remember the look he gave me, I don't recall what he said. I do remember thinking that he was giving me a green light on the idea, whatever that meant. The concept that would become the Lazarus Project for Congregational Renewal was born in my thoughts.

Something else happened during that second session that rocked my confidence and self-esteem. February 14, Valentine's Day, was the second day of the session. Some scamps in the Greensboro church conspired to surprise me. While we were in our small discussion groups, a delivery man came in to deliver a massive balloon bouquet to me. When I called that evening, they told me that they had planned the surprise with the consent of Ed Friedman. They told me he had laughed with them about it.

On Thursday, the last day of the seminar, I approached Ed at lunchtime to talk to him about the surprise. As I began to speak, he said, "Excuse me," and walked across the room to speak to another participant about something. Undeterred, I walked up to him again and started to speak. Once again, he muttered something and walked away. This time, however, he simply crossed the room, turned back and watched me. I realized he was not going to speak to me. This was an intentional snub. Why was he doing this? That afternoon was the first time I asked no questions and made no comments during one of Ed's workshops.

I was so upset by this that, prior to the May workshop, the last one I had signed up for and paid for, I called the counselor who was my small group leader throughout the seminar. After telling her what had happened, I asked if I had done something wrong, if I should stay away from the last workshop for which I had signed up. She expressed that I definitely should attend, that I had a lot to offer and really understood the process.

Perhaps my reaction seems childish, and probably it was. I was bothered by Ed shunning me in large measure because I knew that Ed knew I grasped the Emotional Process paradigm very clearly. That I "got it" when others struggled with it made me feel as if I was due some recognition. Ed never showed that to me, making me wonder if I had been deluding myself. Maybe I wasn't nearly so good at grasping and using Bowen Theory as I thought I was. Perhaps, if I listened more, I would perceive truths and nuances I had been missing. So I decided to attend the last session, though I was unsure of how to act toward Ed and how engaged I should be during the sessions.

The May, 2006, workshop was, like the previous ones, an intriguing experience. I remember that I did make some measured comments and I asked some questions. Ed treated me as he had before, simply like any one of the other students. When the session ended, I waited patiently until I could approach him. I held out my hand and shook his, and I thanked him for his work and for the impact it had on my life and ministry.

Although I put the idea that was to become the Lazarus Project on the back burner, I continued to read Ed's writings and to refine the way I used Family Systems as a pastor. In early October there was a splendidly serendipitous event that caused me to appreciate all that I had learned from Ed about Family Systems. Full of gratitude, I sat down and wrote Ed a letter, sending it to him along with a personalized box of greeting cards. I closed the letter by thanking him for all the changes in my life and work that came as a result of what I had learned from him and his writings. And I wished him a long, productive life in which he might touch the lives of thousands of others just as he had touched mine. I sent the letter about the beginning of the third week of October.

On Halloween, two weeks later, Ed died of a massive heart attack. He was 64.

When the shock of his death began to ebb, I found that I could no longer push aside my intention to begin using Family Systems to revitalize dormant and dying congregations. There was also a tremendous degree of serendipity in my professional life about this time. People came forward to help me sponsor events, to fund our activities and to advise me on writing and publishing the book that emerged: *The Lazarus Project*. The book you're reading is about Emotional Process in families—not about congregations. So, as I have attempted to do throughout the book, I'll keep references to church stuff to a minimum—with one exception. I do want to tell you about my favorite love bomb.

Before I get to that, however, I'd like to conclude my comments about how Dr. Edwin H. Freeman impacted my life directly one last time.

I had been a long distance runner in high school and I came back to it in 1995 when I was 42. Not only did I run five or six times a week, but I took up foot racing. There were a number of folks in the church I pastored who were also runners/racers and they persuaded me to enter the 1998 Marine Corps Marathon. The race was in Washington, D.C., close to where Ed had lived, in October, just before the second anniversary of his death.

Training for the marathon is a lengthy process. It took me about four months to get ready for the race. As you train, you run successively longer distances. As your long training run gets up to 16 or 18 miles, it becomes all the more important to take good care of your lower carriage so as to avoid overuse injuries. Part of my routine after a long run was to dump a sack of ice into the bathtub, fill the tub with water and sit in it until the ice melted.

One particular Saturday morning I got home from a 20 or 22 mile run and found my family was out shopping. So I dumped ice in the tub, ran water over it and sat down in the water, still wearing my running shorts. Because it can take a half an hour or so for the ice to melt, I had a novel with me that I had almost finished: *The Chosen*, by Chaim Potok.

In seminary I had read the marvelous novel *My Name is Asher Lev* by Potok and at that time I had heard about *The Chosen*. I had intended to read the book for nearly 20 years. Somehow this turned out to be the right time to read it. The story is about two Jewish boys. One is Danny Saunders, the son of an Hassidic rabbi. The other is Reuven Malter, the son of an Orthodox Jewish professor. Brought together by forces beyond their control, the boys become friends, only to become disconnected by forces equally beyond their control—religious disagreements between their fathers. Near the end of the book, the religious struggle is resolved and it becomes permissible for the boys to relate to one another again. Reb Saunders, Danny's father, keeps asking his son to invite Reuven to their home. He wants to speak with Reuven. Eventually Reuven overcomes his reluctance and visits the Saunders' home. Throughout the time Reuven had known the Saunders family, he had noticed a phenomenon he could not explain: Reb Saunders did not speak to his son. Apart from asking him questions about the Torah or giving him specific instructions, Reb Saunders did not interact with his eldest child at all. This was doubly strange to Reuven since he knew his friend was *the chosen*: Danny was to take over the Hassidic congregation when his father died.

I sat in the bathtub reading the scene in which Reuven shows up for a last meal at the Saunders' home. Soon Reb Saunders summons the two friends to him and he begins to explain to Reuven, with Danny overhearing, why he does not speak to his son. It was a custom, he said, that the rabbi would not speak directly to the chosen. Thus, he said, the rabbi could not express his profound respect, admiration and love for his son, regardless of how he felt. As he listened, suddenly understanding, Danny wept. As I read, suddenly imagining that perhaps this was why I had been treated as I had by Ed, I sobbed.

About that time my whole family showed up. They heard me crying in the bathroom and came quickly to find me, sitting in ice water, reading an old paperback novel and shaking as I wept. That was hard to explain. At last, however, I got over the way Ed had shunned me. It was like reclaiming my birthright.

Not long after that, I sent an email to Chaim Potok who was then a professor at Penn. In those days, before spam and hacking, you could do that and people would often respond. I told him about my relationship with Ed and how reading his book had been a powerfully transforming event in my life. Chaim Potok responded with a reply email, expressing his gratitude and saying that he had been deeply moved by what I had shared.

One more story, and then we're through.

Christmas of the Special Child

If you read the addendum to this book about the importance of preserving your family's history, you'll recognize from my vignette "No Eggs for Breakfast" that I think it's important to tell family stories *in media res*; that is, tell them as narratives beginning with the tale itself rather than with backstory. Having said that, I'm going to break my own rule and begin describing "The Christmas of the Special Child" with a little introduction.

In 2007 I shut down the Lazarus Project for Congregational Renewal. I did it in part because, as the saying goes, one cannot serve two masters. There were constant demands from churches and leaders around the country for more workshops and consultations with individuals and congregations. Meanwhile I was also busy being a minister, trying to breathe new life into a church I was called to pastor in Winston-Salem, North Carolina. The time had come to choose either to be a topflight consultant or to become the best pastor I could be—and I chose the ministry.

That's partly true. The other reason I shut down Lazarus was because of a nagging awareness I had that I had left something really important out of the curriculum. Oh, everything I wrote in the book, I believe, was accurate and it was correct. The problem was, there was one other truth about healing congregations I had discovered. It was the same sort of truth my middle child encountered soon after he became a Physician's Assistant and began treating patients. He would sometimes call me in great frustration, telling me about patients to whom he poured out his heart in explaining how they could overcome the health problems they were facing. Often he would see them a day or a week later and they were blatantly ignoring his advice.

"I tell you, Dad," he fumed, "if people don't want to get well, you can't force them. If they want to kill themselves slowly, there is nothing you can do about it."

He was right. The best doctor in the world cannot save a patient who is intent on continuing his self-destructive behavior.

Dr. Mike Simpson

Just so, the best church leader in the world cannot breathe new life into a congregation that wants to die. Congregations, indeed, are living things. They make decisions—decisions that are uncanny rather than conscious. They have the uncanny ability to live and thrive. And they have the ability and prerogative to wither and die if that is their actual, underlying desire. These decisions have nothing to do with faith, theology, idealism or rationality, but rather with basic emotion states shared by the congregants. I discovered that my old dictum, "it only takes one person to renew a church," was indeed true—but only half the story. The whole saying should be, "it only takes one person to renew a church that is willing to be renewed."

That was a bitter pill to swallow, but nonetheless a reality that professional caregivers in a multitude of professions have to face. Sometimes, however, a congregation is willing to be renewed and the result is magnificent. And that brings us to the story of my favorite love bomb (so far).

Why didn't we have any kids? When I left the church I pastored in Tulsa, there were 220 adults and 120 children under the age of eighteen. After I had served as pastor for five years at the Greensboro church, our membership was approaching 400, but there were only a couple dozen children.

The Greensboro congregation sought me for dual reasons: 1) to increase the membership and 2) to oversee the building of a new educational wing. We got the educational building built all right, complete with four youth classrooms, a toddler nursery and a crib nursery. And while we added plenty of families over the years—including young couples of child-rearing age—for some reason there weren't many small children. I noted this with great curiosity.

Simultaneously I had begun working with congregation leaders in many other churches and examining the history and stuckness in their congregations. I think it was during the September, 1997, Lazarus workshop that I had a little revelation: the Greensboro church had in its past a multitude of "special children." I use that term here in the broadest sense: children who were born with physical and mental issues; children who died in childhood or developed issues in their childhood that permanently

Fix Your Family

changed their lives; children who experienced life-changing traumas when they were young; adopted children (we had on the order of fifteen or sixteen members who had been adopted as infants over the years from the Children's Home Society). There was one adult Sunday school class of about a dozen families and all but one of those families had a special child in its past. By the time we got through adding up those children through the history of the church that we considered "special," there were more than forty kids. By contrast, the Tulsa church with its overabundance of children had only one child that fit into any of these "special" categories.

I knew the history of the church well enough to know that this unique heritage had never been recognized or celebrated by the congregation as a whole. Accordingly, since the Christmas season was looming, I enlisted a half-dozen helpers and we began to plan a whole Advent season around this topic. The idea was that we were going to celebrate what had never been lifted up or discussed. We called it the "Christmas of the Special Child." We planned to center all our worship services around this topic (beginning with first Sunday in December, in which I preached a sermon about the baby Jesus as an adoptee and a refugee). The worship leaders each Sunday—who gave communion mediations and offered prayers—were parents of special children or even had been special children themselves. We made a list of artifacts around the facility that had been donated in honor or memory of special children: the candlesticks on the communion table, a wall-hanging in one Sunday school room, a globe in the children's wing.

As we entered the Christmas season, we noticed right away a different ambiance surrounding the congregation, a sort of solemn serenity. Each gathering was poignant. The congregation listened with perfect attentiveness to each parent who spoke about the sacredness of this holiday centered around children. One father of a special child, in his communion prayer, spoke of a child whose had died at his father's hand (in the late 50s an enraged, estranged husband burst into his in-laws' home where his wife had taken refuge; he murdered her and his young son, and left his infant daughter unharmed in her crib). In compiling the list of special children, we had forgotten these two. As the season wore on, we found several other instances where we had forgotten children who properly belonged on the list.

One of the older women approached me after the second Sunday and said, "I think I understand why you're doing this, but you better never make us go through this again."

As is the case with some planned nodal events/love bombs, this one caught fire and its scope dramatically expanded. One of my helpers decided it would be a good thing if we recorded the stories of some of these special children. We had their parents write vignettes about the children and compiled them into a booklet, which we duplicated and sent out to the members of the church.

The cover of the booklet came from one of our administrative assistants, who found a beautiful hand drawn picture with the faces of many small children on the internet. She copied it onto the cover. When we sent out the booklet as a mass mailing, immediately another woman in the church charged into the church office and told us that the image we had used was not in the common domain. It had been drawn by an artist in Raleigh and we had used it without permission. The administrator was panicked and wondered what liability we had just incurred. I took a copy of the booklet and mailed it to the artist, explaining our error and asking what we needed to do to make it right. The artist wrote back that she was the mother of a child who had died prematurely and was so pleased that her art serendipitously ended up on the cover of a book about special children.

Another completely serendipitous thing that happened was our Christmas Eve service. I was contacted midway through December by the pastor of a predominantly African-American sister church who wondered if we would be open to their members coming over for our 11 p.m. Christmas Eve service. I explained that we would be delighted, however . . . and I explained what was going on. How would they feel about being part of our focus on the special children? Suddenly we had a partner congregation that was totally invested in what we were doing on Christmas Eve. The pastor asked if one of the members of his church, a mother in her early 30s, could give a meditation before the Christmas offering—which was going to be donated to a children's shelter. Of course we agreed.

I will never forget that service and in particular the lengthy offertory meditation the mother made as she stood on the chancel steps. Three steps down, on the floor of the nave, sat all the children of our sister church intermingled with all the children of our church. Meanwhile the daughter of the mother on the steps, a four-year-old Downs syndrome child, kept climbing up the steps and hugging her mom around the legs, then climbing down the steps, sitting down beside the three-year-old Downs syndrome child of one of the families in our congregation and giving her huge hugs. The mother spoke at length about the miracle that her daughter was to her as we watched this lovely black child alternate between embracing her mother and embracing the other Downs syndrome child who had pure blonde hair and the most spontaneous smile.

That service was theoretically the end of the Christmas of the Special Child, but again, the love bomb just kept expanding. I found that all during the Advent season, apparently confused and thinking we were supporting a specific cause, members and visitors had been giving offerings marked "Christmas of the Special Child." By the time Christmas was over we had nearly $2000 in a fund for which we had no plans.

A couple of new helpers emerged. One was a woman in her forties who had two special siblings in her family; she had grown up taking care of them. The other was a school counselor who tested children in public school and who often had the responsibility of telling parents that their children had learning disabilities. These two decided we should form a Special Child Committee that would use the funds in a variety of ways to assist kids and their families and to educate the public about special needs children. I agreed to this, thinking it would quickly deplete the fund and I wouldn't have to worry about it. Within a year the fund had doubled; whenever a need was suggested, congregants would hear about it and give extra money to cover the expense with the leftovers of their gifts going back to the fund.

A retired minister in the congregation contacted the local newspaper, resulting in an article about our church's history with special children and our new committee that ministered to them. We got a number of requests to assist with special needs for kids. And we also got a slew of families in the community who had been looking for a place where a child with special needs would be welcomed.

Dr. Mike Simpson

There was a wonderful commercial artist in the congregation, a woman who happened to have a special needs grandchild. She sought permission to paint a mural of Noah's Ark with animals trekking toward it in the nursery hallway. To "help" her, she recruited all the willing children of the congregation and oversaw their work as they proudly helped to create this boldly colored masterpiece.

As I indicated before, whenever a nodal event/love bomb is successfully detonated, there are physical results. I guess you could call it "collateral damages?" Anyway, the weekend after we finished the Christmas events, I came down with a high fever out of nowhere. Nobody else seemed to contract it. Forty-eight hours later it was gone. Another of the key helpers was walking across her backyard as she had done every day for decades and unaccountably fell, spraining her ankle badly so that she had to wear a brace for several weeks. Another helper, a woman in her 70s who had been treated for cervical cancer decades before, became alarmed when she suddenly began to exhibit those symptoms again—though it turned out to be a false alarm.

There was one other negative response to the event. Three women in the congregation found their way to the church office at different times, each with a different, severe critique of the Christmas of the Special Child. One, as I wrote above, declared that the church would get sued for the unauthorized use of the cover image. Both of the others had complaints that were minor, but which they pursued with real zest and anger. Being in full "Bowen Theory" mode, I asked myself why these particular women—who did not have reputations for being vitriolic—would be so upset. Then I remembered that each of them was the mother of an adopted child. We had not included the stories of adopted children in the anthology.

Throughout the rest of my tenure at the church, the pervasive attitude was one of joy, accomplishment and anticipation. Just on the basis of the serendipity and the renewed spirit of the congregation, I suppose, I would have considered this love bomb to have been a tremendous success. Ah, but what about the underlying issue that first got me to thinking about where the church might have been stuck?

Beginning in the September following the Christmas of the

Special Child and continuing on for at least the next three years, the congregation experienced a major baby boom. Couples in their 40s who had never brought children into the world began to have kids. A fellow in his early 50s whose wife was in her mid-30s used invitro to bring their first child into the world, then the next year had twins. In those days I conducted more baby dedications than weddings and funerals combined. The nurseries were filled with kids and happy attendants.

Somehow, it seems, the Christmas of the Special Child gave permission to all the potential parents in the church to push aside their reluctance and go for it. Perhaps the legacy of children with problems had created some reserve among potential parents. That season of celebration seemed to convey a more important truth: children are gifts of destiny and caprice, but this was a place where children were welcomed and adored regardless.

About That Subtitle

After reading through all the principles, suggestions and vignettes in this book, you might ask, "Well, how will I know if my family has really been 'fixed?'"

Over the years I've heard variations of that question asked of a number of professors and counselors: "How will I know when I'm well?"

The response that I heard most often was not satisfying or really comprehensible to me for the longest time: "Getting healthy emotionally is like peeling the layers of an onion. When you successfully get one layer off, there is always another layer beneath it to work on."

All the work I've done with my family and the families of others have helped me to understand, however, the threshold for "fixing your family" is both low and high. If you use the insights and methods expressed here and you manage to confront the stuckness in your family such that long-term impediments fall away and to some extent your family is able to grow, to experience new joy, to express affection and to change some of their long-standing negative behaviors, then you have succeeded. You've fixed your family. That does not mean you may not discover new areas of stuckness in the family or that you may recognize new challenges in your own life and in the life of your family. The universe or creation—whatever you want to call it—seems to be set up in such a way that our lives can never be completely "solved," that all potential brokenness and stuckness within us can never completely be "fixed."

    I would note, however, that with every new level of competence we achieve, with every new hurdle we face and overcome, we understand life and relationships just a little bit better. We are more empowered. And we are capable of just a little more joy. Ultimately you must decide for just how much power, peace and happiness you're willing to settle.

Addendum 1
Crisis

Are you in crisis? Do you think it is possible that a few shared thoughts can help you deal with the situation you're facing? What if I said that this paragraph in a small way has already started to help? You ask why?

Because that opening paragraph was entirely made up of questions and questions tend to move the extreme emotions, which invariably accompany any crisis, toward the mental background as they draw your thinking processes to the fore. Being able to think rationally about the crisis you're in is the first step back from panic, the first step toward making logical decisions that aren't clouded by your emotions. Right now, perhaps, this is an important thing for you.[xxxvii]

Being in crisis means you really can't fully focus on anything else until the situation is dealt with in some meaningful way. We are conscious of that reality and sympathetic to it. While each crisis is unique in many ways, we would also observe that pretty much every crisis has certain common characteristics. For that reason, we wanted to share four observations about crises in general.

•*You do not **solve** a crisis; instead you **manage** it*. Whenever we find ourselves in crisis, our greatest desire to get out of it, to return our lives to normal, to undo the negative reality that threw us into crisis. If what we were facing was a problem we could fix, however, we wouldn't be in crisis. You can't "solve" a car accident or a heart attack or a child overdosing on drugs. What you can do is manage the situation to the best of your ability, make the best available decisions and don't allow your emotions to lure you into impetuous actions as the situation sorts itself out. Perhaps the key here is to be patient with yourself and the situation as your work to return balance to your life.

•*This too shall pass*. One comment that has always seemed *least* helpful to me in the midst of a crisis is for someone to say that it will pass—but it will. This little proverb is constantly used among members of the 12 Step movement (Alcoholics Anonymous, Al Anon, Narcotics Anonymous, etc.). By definition, one has to have lived through some life-changing crises to qualify for a 12 Step group. This is not to say that the crisis will end with a blissful, perfect outcome or that there is a set time it will conclude, but the simple reality is that every crisis that turns our world upside down will eventually come to an end. So, as is also said among 12 Step adherents, don't give up before the miracle.

•*The most important and first question to ask when you find yourself in a crisis, is "What is the best way this can work out for me and how can I help to bring that about?"* This probably sounds sort of mercenary and selfish, but I say this because so often family leaders and caregivers go to great lengths and make profound personal sacrifices for other family members, only to end up bearing most of the stress and anxiety associated with the situation. I'm going to make the cruel suggestion that you look out for number one—that is, look out for yourself—as a priority. That doesn't necessarily mean others in your family will suffer because of your selfishness. It simply means that you make sure you don't bear more than your share of the emotional toll of the crisis.

•*Ask yourself if the roots of this crisis were present in your family before it happened and, once the crisis is over, is the potential for other, similar disasters still present.* Obviously, if an asteroid lands on your house, it's pretty unlikely anyone in your family did anything to cause that directly or indirectly. If, however, a heavy smoker in your family has a heart attack; if there had been growing emotional distance between yourself and your spouse and your spouse up and leaves; if your teenage daughter had been isolating and giving away her favorite possessions before her suicide attempt, as the crisis is approaching resolution it's important to ask, "Are those contributing factors still present?" During the time of crisis, you may not be able to address those issues, but, once the smoke clears, dealing with those contributing factors may go a long way to preventing future problems.

Please know that the casual comments in this brief addendum are not an indication that we take any crisis lightly. We don't. Crisis may be defined as one's world turned on its head, something that is not pleasant and not funny. Our hope is that all the resources you'll need to face your unique situation will be available to you and that the peace of emotional balance will return to you, your family and the world around you. We hope as well that, in overcoming the significant problem you're now facing, you'll find strength and understanding that will stand with you in days ahead should you face any crisis again.

Dr. Mike Simpson

Addendum 2
Preserving Yesterday for Tomorrow

No Eggs for Breakfast

Margie came back from the henhouse empty handed.

Glancing up from the stove, where she was frying bacon, Bertha asked, "Where are the eggs?"

The ten-year-old shrugged. "There weren't any eggs, Mom."

"No eggs?" Bertha stared at her eldest daughter. Then understanding lit her face. "Oh.... Margie, hand me the broom."

As her mother slid the skillet off the burner and wiped her hands, Margie pulled the straw broom from the corner. Purposely striding out the kitchen door, Bertha grabbed the broom and headed down the hill toward the coop. Margie, now exceedingly curious, followed a step behind her mother.

The absence of eggs for Bertha and her young family was no small thing. She and her husband were subsistence farmers, trying to feed five children in the early years of the Depression. Their dozen dependable hens provided the daily bounty of eggs they counted on for breakfast and baking. Having no eggs for breakfast, therefore, was a significant setback.

Inside the henhouse, Bertha ignored the flapping, perturbed chickens. She studied the upper angles of the little structure. There was a small ledge made of two-by-fours running all the way around the top, just beneath the ceiling. Bertha began to sweep the bristles of the broom along that ledge as if she were dusting the upper reaches of the henhouse. Halfway round, she encountered an obstruction. With a mighty swat, she pushed the impediment off the ledge. A long, fat blacksnake sailed through the air and hit the floor of the henhouse. Lying in the dust and feathers of the wooden floor, the round shapes of a half dozen eggs inside the snake were obvious.

Margie and the snake were equally stunned. Before the girl could scream—or the serpent could retreat—Bertha snatched its tail and proceeded to pound it, whip-like, against the floor.

Fix Your Family

"If I—can't have—the eggs," she cried fiercely as she whacked the snake again and again, "you—can't have—the eggs!"

Bertha Simpson, my father's mother, was a tiny woman who lived a huge life. Born in 1898, Grandma lived ninety-six tumultuous, triumphant years. She outlived two husbands and raised fourteen of her sixteen children to adulthood. In the words of my Uncle Ronny, she was "tough as whet leather." Despite her fierce fearlessness, however, her children and her forty-two grandchildren all remembered her as a tender and compassionate, wise and loving.

The one other quality her descendants would all ascribe to her was "storyteller." My earliest memories of Grandma involved sitting beside her for hours and listening to tales of my father's childhood, of the two world wars, of farm and family and the grandfather I never met.

I also remember her children encouraging her to "write down those stories, Mom." The older she grew, the more insistent they became. When at last she was living in a retirement home, one of her sons brought her a tape recorder and instructed her to begin reciting all her precious stories into the microphone. By then, unfortunately, it was too late. Grandma had lost the focus that allowed her to spin her wonderful tales coherently. Much of the grief we all felt over her death in 1994 was because of the loss of her stories, our connection to her magnificent life. The story above—about the blacksnake and the eggs—was related to me by my Aunt Margie, not by Grandma.

My dad in particular was affected by our failure to capture a meaningful record of Grandma's life, or even her retelling the nodal events, the milestone moments. A couple times in previous chapters, I mentioned Dad and I taking a "cemetery tour" of our family's gravesites. We stared at the tombstones of relatives—people of whom we had never heard, yet who bore our surname and were buried alongside other kinfolk—and wondered who they were, what they did, who their descendants were. We shared a sense of yearning to know about them—our people, cut off from any possibility of sharing their stories with us.

Though he was not the storyteller his mother was, after the famous "love bomb" on the road back from Heathen Ridge, Dad vowed he would write down his memories and family history so the coming generations of his family would know firsthand about these relatives of theirs who had passed from the world. Eventually he did get around to procuring a digital voice recorder with the intention of preserving his stories. By then, caught in the mid-stages of Alzheimer's, he too had lost his opportunity to record what was most precious to him.

Having lived through this phenomenon twice, I made the determination I would not wait until it was too late to record for those coming generations—my family and others who might be interested—that which has been most precious to me in my life. Moreover, beyond simply fulfilling my determination to write down my family history and the remembrances shared with me, I have become an emissary—a sort of literary prophet—on behalf of all the unrecorded family histories out there just waiting to be written down. And my prophetic message is this: You know those stories you've had for so long and how you thought, "Someday I should write that down?" Well I've come to tell you the time is at hand: **write it down while you can**. I'm fortunate to say that I have completed a memoir and given my children each a copy.

During the writing of this book I regularly handed off completed chapters to my loyal editors and proofers. When those chapters came back to me with corrections and comments, I would ask my readers for their opinion about what I had written. The most common comment I received was, "It got me thinking about my family and I was amazed at what I didn't know about them."

There are other cultures—and I think this was true of our society in times past—in which preserving the stories of ancestors in each new generation is a requirement. I guess the most obvious example of this is the famous family history called *Roots* by Alex Haley. Haley's predecessors used oral history to preserve the stories of their deceased relatives going all the way back to the enslavement of a young man named Kunta Kinte in Gambia in 1767. It was a desire to remain connected to their ancestral home that drove this family to teach their history to each successive generation. Many, many different societies have made the preservation of family, clan and cultural history a priority.

To me, this is a great irony. Today's generations are living in the midst of the most radical changes, developments, migratory shifts and social upheaval in human history. No age ever had more intriguing, exciting things to share than ours. And, never has humanity had so many options for recording our personal and shared histories. Somehow, however, preserving our history for coming generations is not a priority. Specifically, families on the whole do not seem interested in keeping records of their shared lives. I cannot stress strongly enough, **we need to create and pass down the history of who we were, what we did and why we did it for those generations yet unborn**. There are few greater bequests we can make for our progeny than to share the record of ourselves when we have passed from the scene.

Earlier in this book I described a scene from the motion picture *Saving Private Ryan*. That movie opens with an older man, his family trailing behind him, walking through the grave markers of an American military cemetery in France. Among those accompanying him are two granddaughters in their mid-teen years. They are presented as giggly and totally disconnected from the significance of where they are. That is yet another way in which the movie is quite realistic. Adolescent children are not capable of grasping the poignancy and gravity of a military graveyard. On the other hand, the movie was released in 1998. By the time of this writing, the girls in that scene would be in their 30s, probably with children of their own. The cemetery tour they took with their grandfather would have acquired a whole new depth of meaning, especially if their grandfather, who it turns out was the Private Ryan of the movie's title, explained to them why he searched out that particular grave marker.

We all have stories we've heard, experiences we lived and truths we've learned that we can share with those who come after us, after we're gone. Either we save what is most precious and leave it for the coming generations, or it will be lost. My advice, for what it's worth, is that you take what you knew and what you've learned about your family and record it. We live in an age of simple, inexpensive recording devices: smart phones, voice recorders and digital video recorders whose files can be saved in multiple formats and locations. It is astonishingly easy to self-publish a family history in book form. I cannot encourage you enough to save your story for those days after you're gone.

Dr. Mike Simpson

Index

Ability to Anticipate: 89
Anxiety: 60, 75, 92, 102-106
Anxiety Football: 104
Birth Family: 10
Birthday Party Revisited, The: 107, 133
Bound/Fused, 31
Bowen, Murray: 56, 97, 127, 132, 145
Bowen Theory: 98, 127
Cascade Effect: 133f
Cemetery Tours: 41
Chaim Potok:150f
Chosen, The: 150f
Christmas of the Special Child,The: 152ff
Chronic Conflict: 32, 44
Circle-Back Question/Columbo Question: 39
Conflict Scale: 30, 33, 44
Connection: 105ff
Conspiracy: 62ff
Crisis: 1f, 160f
Cut-Off/Estranged: 28, 31
Denial: 58, 67, 72
Differentiated: 77
Distance Scale: 30, 44
Embrace and Fuse: 93f
Emotional Balance: 55ff, 68ff
Emotional Process: 8, 19ff, 31, 56,72,74, 76, 90, 92, 137, 145f
Extended Family: 10
False Information: 58, 72
Family Constellation: 71f
Family Gram: 24ff
Family of Origin: 10
Family Saga: 46
Family Systems: 73, 97, 145ff
Friedman, Edwin H.: 47, 60, 75f, 91, 95ff, 102, 112, 133, 136

Gossip: 100f
Homeostasis: 55
Lazarus Project for Congregational Renewal, The: 133, 137, 148f
Leadership: 77, 84, 86f, 91, 110, 146
Lundblad, Dennis: 14
Love Bomb: 112f, 116, 121f, 124, 126f, 132, 141, 153
Negation: 91, 110
Nodal Event: 112f, 121, 126, 133, 136, 139, 155, 157
Nuclear Family: 10
Opposition: 91
Paradoxical Intent/ Reversal: 98f, 100, 110
Patience: 88ff
Patterns/Themes: 28, 43, 46f, 49ff, 55f, 72
Persistence: 87ff
Physics of Human Relationships: 70, 72
Playfulness: 95ff
Pursuit: 71, 86
Questions: 33, 35ff, 44, 59, 87, 100, 114ff, 151, 160
River of Emotion 15, 21
Sabotage: 91ff
Secrets: 58, 62ff, 65, 72
Seriousness: 95ff, 110
Shlemiel/ Shlimazel: 92
Stuckness: 21f, 30, 49, 77, 84f, 87, 94f, 110, 112f, 116f, 121, 124, 132f, 138, 141, 158f
Super Reasonable: 32, 44
Taboo Subjects: 25, 58, 67, 72
Triangles: 68ff
Uncanny Conspiracy: 66f
Well-Defined: 77, 84, 110, 137, 146

Dr. Mike Simpson

For Further Reading

Bowen, Murray, *Family Therapy in Clinical Practice*, Roman and Littlefield, 1985

centerforfamilyprocess.com
[This is the website of the institute established by Edwin H. Friedman that continues to perpetuate his work directly; excerpts and other writings are available on this site.]

Friedman, Edwin H., *Friedman's Fables*, Guilford, 1990

Friedman, Edwin H., *Generation to Generation: Family Process in Church and Synagogue*, Guilford, 1985

Kerr, Michael E. and Bowen, Murray, *Family Evaluation*, W.W. Norton, 1988

McGoldrick, Monica, *You Can Go Home Again*, [Reprinted as *The Genogram Journey*], W.W. Norton, 1995

[There are actually a great many books now available that focus on Bowen Theory/Family Systems, including many that deal specifically with the family and family issues. The books listed here have been selected as a group of basic texts that deal with the background and underlying concepts of the topics covered in this book.]

Endnotes

[i] For our purposes, we are going to assume there are ten basic emotions, five we experience as negative and five as positive. In the same way that all visible colors are some combination of three primary colors (red, blue and yellow), all emotional states are some combination of these six emotions: anger, fear, sadness, yearning, pain; joy, love, sex, fulfillment, pleasure.

[ii] To keep things sort of straight: **birth family** = Mom, Dad, siblings; **family of origin** = grandparents, aunts & uncles and the crowd your parents came from (your parents' birth families); **extended family** = everyone who by blood, marriage, adoption or habit has come to be included emotionally as part of your clan; **nuclear family** = the people with whom you live or whom you brought into the world at some point and their descendants and significant others.

[iii] Actually I really dislike the word "iteration," so I decided to use the word once in the book and get it over with . . . well, twice if you want to count this end note.

[iv] The movie was based on the book *The Whale Rider*, by Witi Ihimaera, Reed Books, 1987.

[v] You can break this down even more into additional, more intense family groups. Take for instance your house of worship: the people who attend the 8:30 service are a family; the people in your religious education small group are a family; the widows in the congregation are a family. The same is true of any other large organization to which you belong.

[vi] Yes, before I hear from naturalists everywhere, I do know that bound water bodies and wetlands also are living things.

[vii] Before you ask, yes, this is a true story, as are all the vignettes and case studies that originate with me in this book. Names and specifics in each instance have been changed to conceal the identities of those I describe. The people, events and outcomes, however, are all true and accurate.

[viii] By way of disclaimer, allow me to say that we in no way mean to demean or discount the role of the physician and/or the therapist in dealing with emotional well-being. Clearly there are individuals who suffer pathologies of such a nature that the only available help capable of making at least a palliative impact are medication and institutionalized mental health care. It may be the case, also, that the longer emotional or physical impairment—such as addiction, for instance—persists, the more it becomes imprinted on the individual in question and the less malleable such folks are to the sort of family emotional processes we are utilizing in *Fix Your Family*. Whatever the case, it can be said with certainty that this is an area requiring more scientific investigation.

Dr. Mike Simpson

[ix] Most of us don't think about "literary devices," but there are many different kinds and they have distinct purposes. For example, we all know that a *limerick* is a five-line rhyming poem intended to make us laugh. A *myth* is an epic story whose purpose is to explain grand underlying truths about human existence. Parables are intended to challenge our conventional understanding of the world by upsetting our comfortable assumptions and opinions. A fairly well-known example of a parable is *Crash*, the movie that won the 2004 Academy Award for Best Picture; *Crash* systematically exposes and confronts the prejudices of virtually every person in its extensive cast, revealing all their prejudices to be false and hurtful. Another interesting example is *The Green Mile*, a novel and later movie that describes a number of paradoxes: a life-giving healer chooses to accept his own unjust execution because he has grown weary of the pain and injustice he has experienced; a man given the gift of a long, healthy life eventually perceives it to be a curse. Maybe the greatest irony about this collection of parables is that it's written by Stephen King, who is generally regarded as an author of gruesome horror tales.

[x] These simple line drawings are typically called "genograms": pictures of the various generations of your family. I like "family gram" because it stresses the fact it's family you're investigating. And also because sticking the syllable "gram" on the end of it makes it sound like a message you're sending your family, like a telegram or a flower-gram: "Love gram for the Smith family." Yes, I know they don't deserve it . . . yet.

[xi] I recall working with a student who wanted to understand herself as a psychologist would. "What kind of person am I?" she asked. "I'll let you decide," I said, and started listing the characteristics of the various personality adaptations. After we went through the basic personality types, she frowned. "That's it?" she blurted. "Am I on that list? I thought you would finally get around to 'normal.'" I laughed. "They are all 'normal.' There are a lot of different ways to be 'normal.'"

[xii] Active listening comes easier to some of us than others, but any of us can learn it. The key is to pay attention so you can feed back in other words what you've heard. John says to you angrily, "My wife Mary spends money without any consideration of our budget! She's going to bankrupt us!" As an active listener, you might respond, "You're worried Mary is going to cause financial ruin because she's irresponsible with your money." Active listening doesn't mean you've taken sides or that you agree or disagree. It's just a way of demonstrating that you understand what you've been told.

[xiii] A "loaded child" as I use the term refers to a family member who,

from birth or before, has some special significance to the family, a significance that plays itself out over the course of the life of the family. Joseph Kennedy, Jr., the namesake of his extremely driven father, was a loaded child—the person his father intended to be President of the United States. When Joe Jr. was killed in World War II, those expectations shifted to Joe's younger brother, John F. Kennedy. Many things can result in a person becoming a "loaded child": childhood trauma, birth order, drama during pregnancy and so forth.

[xiv] I've come to appreciate an acronym applied to the word "denial," used often with those recovering from drug addiction: "Denial means 'Don't Even Know I Am Lying.'"

[xv] In investigating my father's family, I discovered that my Uncle Leslie was only one of three people in his generation for whom there had never been a memorial service. No funeral was held for my Uncle Floyd, who was killed in Germany in World War II and subsequently buried in France. No funeral was held for, Rhonda, the stillborn infant twin sister of my Uncle Ronny. When I suggested to my cousin, Leslie's oldest child—who was himself then in his 60s—that we have a memorial service for these three siblings, my cousin replied with alarm, "But we can't hold a funeral for my dad! What if he comes back?" This was more than fifty years after his father's disappearance and the occasion of anyone hearing from him. I was amazed at the persistence of the denial being expressed.

[xvi] There is an old saying that there are those topics about which a great deal must be said, or very little must be said. As we were outlining the material for this book, we wrestled the subject of adulterous affairs; either we had to have an entire chapter or maybe even a second volume dedicated to it, or we were going to confine our comments to a footnote. You can see which won out. Our decision was based on the notion that we didn't want this topic to overwhelm the overall direction of the book. Still, there are several brief observations we'd like to make, some of which may be difficult to read if you have or are in the middle of dealing with a spouse/partner who has had or is having an affair. 1) If you are trying to work on a marriage or committed relationship and the other person is having an affair, you are very unlikely to make progress while that affair is ongoing; if and when that relationship is resolved and you still want to work on yours, then progress is possible. 2) While it is an extremely difficult thing to do, paradoxical intent, a reversal, is by far the most effective means of confronting a person who is having an affair. Actually emotionally pushing the person who is having the affair toward his/her correspondent is the most likely means of finding resolution. This

implies allowing the person to whom you wish to be committed the freedom to face her/his own behavior and make a decision. Once that decision is made, the next steps are usually fairly obvious. 3) Affairs in our research have turned out almost always to be "secondary behaviors." In the same way that anger is a secondary emotion (whenever you realize you are feeling angry, the reality is you were experiencing [perhaps consciously or subconsciously] some other, powerful emotion prior to your anger), so an affair belies a different, prior issue. While you may be devastated about the affair itself, finding the underlying reason and dealing with that is actually ultimate solution to this betrayal of trust.

[xvii] Weird, isn't it? By definition an uncanny conspiracy is unintended, yet it has a definite purpose; I think we can say that uncanny conspiracies have emotional rather than rational intentionality.

[xviii] Among those who study and utilize the principles of Family Systems/Emotional Process, this quality is typically referred to as "self-differentiation"; to be self-differentiated from others around you is perceived to be one of the most important characteristics of the successful leader.

[xix] One of the brightest, highest-achieving people I know is a woman who also happens to be one of the best-defined individuals I've ever encountered. When I expressed my admiration for her ability to decide for herself what and how she was going to proceed through life, not allowing herself to be cajoled or manipulated by all the strong personalities around her, her response was, "Well you know, I learned at an early age that people tell you you're being good when you're doing the things *they* want you to do. It's amazing how much peace of mind comes from doing what *you* think is right yourself, then letting other people decide if they agree with what you've done."

[xx] It's not all that unusual for dramatic changes in the routines of a family to occur "naturally," that is, without anyone planning for or anticipating they will happen. Sudden, unexpected death (which, incidentally, is another theme that runs in my family), the loss of a job, an unplanned pregnancy, a physical health crisis: these are all events that can of their own accord dramatically, completely alter the pathway a family is traveling.

[xxi] This is a direct quote from Ed Friedman's magnum opus, *Generation to Generation*. I remember the first time I read those words. I was working in a place where I was doing a good job, but getting roundly, constantly criticized. Suddenly I realized the criticism was less about my failures, but rather about the unmet emotional needs of the people who were attacking me.

[xxii] Back when I was a pastor, a church member named Larry called me one Sunday afternoon (first indication that something is up: this guy never called me for any reason) and complimented me on a fine sermon. After I thanked him, he said, "I only wish I could have heard it, what with those two obnoxious little boys sitting in front of us. Hasn't anybody told that lady we have a church nursery?" The typical, pastoral thing to do would have been to promise you would have someone contact the woman and ask her if she would take her children to the nursery during worship (second indication: Larry and his wife sat behind that mother and her sons every Sunday and the kids were always obnoxious—and she ignored requests to take them to the nursery). I agreed with Larry that this was a problem and spent a couple of minutes talking about respecting worship and trying to teach people about proper decorum. Then I asked, "Wow, Larry, we haven't talked in a while. How are things going with you?" Instantly his whole tone changed and he told me that during the prior week he had been passed over for a job promotion that went instead to a fellow he had trained. Larry was devastated. We spent about twenty minutes talking about that, which, of course, was the real reason for his call. The moral to the story is: the less valid the criticism you are receiving is, the more likely something else is going on with the person who is criticizing you.

[xxiii] One of the proverbial cautions we've used when it comes to creating lasting, meaningful change is: "Everything works for two weeks." Stuckness is not only resilient, it's patient as well. Stuckness will let you try out every new diet, every new study guide, every self-help guru's expensive program for enlightenment and financial gain and—surprise—everything works! For two weeks, or until your emotional resolve weakens. Then the same patterns of stuckness reemerge, and you discover nothing has actually changed. Most new programs, solutions, methods, etc., are really an attempt to stick new veneer on something that cannot support or sustain it. The reason *Fix Your Family* works is in that it attacks the root of the old issue rather than trying to varnish it over with something shiny and new.

[xxiv] In our work, we've gotten in habit of calling such appeals the "CRR," the *Carefully Reasoned Response*; about the CRR we make this observation: it invariably fails and the person making the response always seems to be stunned that the people whom she/he is addressing don't "get it." The CRR fails because it is a logical response to an emotion problem.

[xxv] One of the most common phenomena I witnessed among churches and other declining organizations over the years is that those in charge

will bring in a dynamic person and charge him/her with the responsibility of renewing the organization. Then those who hired this new change agent proceed to dump tons of obligations onto her/him, generally in proportion to the new person's desire to bring about the requested change. This is an effort on the part of the family/group to maintain emotional balance—even in the face of the death of the organization.

[xxvi] By the way, the less mature a person is, the more likely that person will win any battle of wills. And no one ever won a battle of wills with a teenager; they just "go underground," resort to "guerilla warfare" and work to find the most painful way to make the life of the adults around them miserable.

[xxvii] I think it's important to be sincere in one's willingness to be connected and not just posturing or being "theoretical." It's always irritated me to hear people totally condemn other individuals or groups and then proclaim, "I say this in all love." I perceive that to be "theoretical" love as opposed to "actual" love. Actual love says, "You know, I have a difficult time with your beliefs (or actions, politics, religion, whatever), but I respect you as a person and I would like to remain a part of your life." It says that out loud, not theoretically. Say it aloud to someone and it is an invitation to connectedness.

[xxviii] Criticism is a form of pursuit. Surely you didn't forget that, right?

[xxix] We are all familiar with the concept of a "catastrophe." Most of us are not familiar with the idea of a "eucatastrophe," which can be defined literally as a "catastrophe of good." The destruction of the Berlin Wall was a eucatastrophe, as was the discovery of the smallpox vaccine, the invention of the air conditioner and the birth of Abraham Lincoln. Note that some of those events were planned or the result of intentional endeavor, whereas others were purely accidental. Just as there can be a multitude of bad explosions, so there can be explosions of goodness—some coincidental and others the result of intentional action.

[xxx] The French have a proverb: "All men have good reasons for the things they do." I bring this up as a way of saying that, whatever misery and injustice has been heaped upon you by members of your own family had some sort of purpose behind it at the time it happened—maybe wrongheaded, ignorant and hostile, but still there was a reason. An essential part of helping your family to become unstuck is in forgiving them for having flawed reasons for the hurtful things they have done. And as long as I'm sermonizing, I'd like to point out that there is a limited amount of justice available in our world; mercy, however, abounds if you will accept and extend it.

[xxxi] When teenagers and other emotionally poorly defined individuals say, "I hate you! I never want to see you again!" they mean for, like, fifteen

minutes. The rest of us mean it for longer periods of time, but very seldom do we actually mean "never." You may note that on those occasions when we say, "I never want to see you again," and we really do mean it and that pronouncement does last for a lifetime, we are usually not very emotional at all.

[xxxii] Ed Friedman in *Generation to Generation* warned leaders of the danger of being "anxiously helpful."

[xxxiii] As a kid, I faithfully searched many an atlas of the western half of the U.S. looking for Northfolk, but I never found it. I've just about come to the conclusion that it wasn't a real place. I think maybe they just made it up for the TV show.

[xxxiv] I think this probably leads to a discussion of the whole idea of "motivation" and "momentum." Very often we see dynamic changes, new ideas, new determination and new results spring forth from the same group of people when the emotional dynamic changes. Maybe the key element in creating new success and finding more productive directions isn't so much "thinking outside the box," as it is "receiving emotional empowerment."

[xxxv] We should also note that a lot of physically positive things result from acquiring the ability to utilize Emotional Process. For instance, one fellow who studied with us had been told by his orthopedic surgeon that he had to have double hip replacement. About this time he began to use Family Systems professionally and in his personal life. In the peaceful new attitude he acquired, he decided to take long walks in order to prepare himself for his upcoming surgery. Living in Blue Ridge Mountains, he found himself walking up hills and then, amazingly, climbing mountain paths. Eventually he did go back to the orthopedic surgeon, but only to show off his perfectly mended hip joints.

[xxxvi] After I wrote my essay about the TLG, I sent a copy of it to Ed, thanking him for writing *Generation to Generation* and expressing the profound change it brought about in my leadership. While he never responded personally to me, he did refer an area Tulsa pastor to me as a Family Systems colleague, expressing the opinion that I "seemed to understand the process." From Ed, that was the highest praise.

[xxxvii] In the world of ironies, this fits right in. Just as I started writing this section, I received a phone call from a young mom whose son, a fourteen-year-old living with his father in another state, had suffered a bad experience when he experimented with a certain illegal drug for the first time. She was beside herself, emotionally thrashing about and totally at a loss as to how to respond. I wasn't sure either, but I did know that if I kept asking her questions, the emotional fog around her would diminish,

which it did. By the next morning, the crisis wasn't over, but the necessary next direction for her was much clearer.

www.ingramcontent.com/pod-product-compliance
Lightning Source LLC
Chambersburg PA
CBHW070850050426
42453CB00012B/2116